'I have had the privilege of being p
births and the name selection proc
me as mothers and fathers deliberate on choosing the most
appropriate and best name for their newborn babies.
This is the much-awaited book that will increase the
understanding of why names are so important.
Sonia's guidance is fantastic as appropriate names will
expand the energy field of the babies to give them a life full
of love, abundance, laughter and fulfilment.'

**Dr Marie Gowri Motha**, author and midwife


'In her book, *Choose The Perfect Baby Name*, Sonia Ducie fires
you a clear and subtle overview of what is in a name, so that
you can choose the best names for your precious offspring,
friends, pets and even for yourself.'

**Claudine Aegerter**, author and founder of Connaissance
School of Numerology


'I consulted Sonia about the naming of my daughter Lily
because I wanted to give her the best start in life. Sonia gave me
great reassurance by confidently counselling me about the
spelling of her name. I never forgot her advice and eight years
later, she was able to give me instant and startlingly accurate
insight into her character development just from her name.'

**Tanith Carey**, author and journalist

'I found choosing a name for my little girl a big responsibility, but there was an aspect of comfort in my Numerology reading from Sonia. She opened my eyes to what kind of character might inhibit her name. A name is the first gift you bestow on your child and to me the brilliance of Numerology is that it helps you to make an informed choice.'

**Samantha Roddick**, human rights activist

## About the Author

Sonia Ducie, Dip CSN AIN, is the best-selling author of 12 Numerology books (translated into 14 languages). She has been giving Numerology readings, workshops, professional training, and presenting business seminars for more than 17 years.

## Qualifications

Member, Association Internationale de Numerologues (AIN)
Diploma Connaissance School of Numerology (CSN)
Connaissance School Teacher (CST)

## Other books by the same author

*Numerology: Your Personal Guide for Life*

*Power Pendants: Wear Your Lucky Numbers Every Day*

*Do It Yourself Numerology: How to Unlock the Secrets of Your Personality with Numbers*

*Numerology (Collins Gem)*

*Sonia Ducie's Numerology Secrets: Find Success and Happiness in Love, Sex and Work*

*The Complete Illustrated Guide to Numerology: Using the Language of Numbers as a Personal Life Guide*

*The Lucky Numbers Oracle: Discover the Power of Numerology*

*Numerology: Your Love and Relationship Guide*

*Directions for Life: Numerology*

*The Principles of Numerology*

*The Self-Help Reflexology Handbook: Easy Home Routines for Hands and Feet to Enhance Health and Vitality*

# Choose the Perfect Baby Name

Use numerology to decide on a name
that will benefit your child for life

## Sonia Ducie
Dip CSN AIN

WATKINS PUBLISHING
LONDON

This edition first published in the UK and USA 2011 by
Watkins Publishing, Sixth Floor, Castle House,
75–76 Wells Street, London W1T 3QH

Text Copyright © Sonia Ducie 2011

1 3 5 7 9 10 8 6 4 2

Designed by Jerry Goldie

Printed in India by Imago

British Library Cataloguing-in-Publication Data Available

Library of Congress Cataloging-in-Publication Data Available

ISBN: 978-1-907486-52-4

www.watkinspublishing.co.uk

Distributed in the USA and Canada by Sterling Publishing Co., Inc.
387 Park Avenue South, New York, NY 10016-8810


For information about custom editions, special sales, premium and
corporate purchases, please contact Sterling Special Sales
Department at 800-805-5489 or specialsales@sterlingpub.com

*I dedicate this book*
*to all the new baby souls of this world.*
*May you always walk your talk,*
*keep love in your heart,*
*and the light in your life.*

# Contents

# Introduction

I profoundly believe that those who take responsibility for themselves and the world live the longest. During infancy everyone knows the importance of feeding a baby the right foods, and from week to week when the newborn is weighed, even the slightest imbalance is pointed at parents by the medical profession. Is the baby not being fed, or being overfed? What kind of food is the precious one eating? Ooh – the responsibility. The baby's growth depends primarily on the love it receives and the physical nourishment it takes in order to survive.

Later on in childhood, young ones categorically let their parents know what they like or dislike. However, childhood conditioning is absolute and parents or immediate family influence their children's behaviour generally for life.

When a child reaches teenage years and on into their 20s they learn to take responsibility for their feelings and their emotional reactions to the world. Later on the child-now-adult learns to take responsibility for their thoughts (which affect all their actions), and for their intellectual understanding of the world. Spiritual responsibility comes into play when an adult recognizes there's more to life than self – we are all one. Once we can recognize the unity, collective responsibility comes into play. There is a natural desire to want to preserve life by respecting the planet, recycling our goods, sharing our resources, and taking care of one another's needs.

Many prospective parents avoid having children due to the responsibilities involved, and that's a choice. But responsibilities are humanity's lifeline; they help us to grow, and they bear great gifts if we are prepared to take up the challenge.

My parents William and Agnes enjoyed the challenge when choosing my First Name. Initially they were both set on two options – Linda or Sonja (my mother favoured the Russian spelling with a 'j'). However, my father registered 'Sonia' spelt with an 'i', the English way, on my birth certificate. As a Numerologist I can see they were both right; Linda and Sonia (with an 'i', my dad's choice) both add up to 22/4, and so I got what I needed.

My dad's Pet Name for me was 'Little Toots' – more divine synchronicity. Little adds up to 24/6 (the same as my surname Ducie). Toots adds up to 17/8 (the same as my Year of Birth); together these Pet Names add up to 41/5 (the exact number of my soul vibration). Clever work.

Naming a child is an enormous responsibility, and the whole process is completely mind-boggling and fascinating. It is always a privilege to help parents find the best potential names for their babies.

Love and Light,

Sonia

Part One

# The Power in a Name

Chapter 1

# What's in a Name, What's in a Number?

Choose the *Perfect Baby Name* is intended to be an essential guidebook for all you parents, to help you make the best possible choice for your baby's names. Numerology provides a very accurate weather forecast that highlights the best potential, but predicting how someone or something will turn out is quite another matter! As parents you can give your child the best start in life by choosing the right names, and then it's up to them to explore their potential, and for you to step back and see what they make out of their lives. Numerology taps into your intuition and brings you seeds of truth, and as parents you can learn to listen because you know what's best and what feels right. However, as parents it's reassuring to note that the classical interpretations of names passed down throughout the ages are identical to the very qualities and meanings revealed in the Numerology of names.

In the past, naming a child was so easy. If your father was a cook or baker then his Family Name or Surname was likely to be Baker or Cook, and you would have taken on this name too.

Similarly, if the mother was always happy her children were likely to be called Merry or Joy as First Names, for example, reflecting the mother's sunny characteristics. If a family lived near woods, then they may have been called The Wood Family but even today parents call their children names based upon where they live or where their baby was conceived. For example, Bristol, Paris or Brooklyn. However, at that time mankind was living a very simple life compared to today, which was reflected in their choice of names. Trends in babies' names form an outer reflection of the soul consciousness of humanity at any given time, which is why some baby names remain popular for centuries and others don't stick around for long.

So what's in a name ... Sophie, Jack, Mother Teresa, Marks & Spencer, Tiffany? Names are incredibly powerful vibrations. Numerology allows you to gain deep insights into the true meaning of any name vibration. It enables you to delve into the sound and go beyond into soul and intuition. Numerology enables you to tap into the subconscious energy behind the physical sound you hear, or the names you read. Each letter forms a musical note, and by translating each letter into a number from the alphabet (A=1, B=2, C=3, and so on) you can feel its true vibration, and feel its inner meaning or intent.

Numerology is an ancient tool that enables you to explore your inner make-up and also helps you to understand the outer world. The Numbers 1 to 9 contain infinite potential for personal and collective transformation and healing. That's because each time you travel through a 9 cycle, you end up back at 1 (10 is reduced to 1+0=1), wiser from all the experiences and lessons you've learned from the previous cycle. Each number highlights positive strengths (qualities which you may recognize) and shadow qualities (some hidden, some you may not recognize and others you may not want to see or address).

Sounding your own name and hearing it repeated by others can help you make contact with your true self, so that you can be more at one with yourself, and come home so that you can be yourself. When others' names are sounded it makes you feel comfortable or it can leave you feeling ill at ease. Indeed, some names or sound vibrations resonate with you, and you say you like that person or place. Other name vibrations grate against you so you shut off your ears or walk away. It may feel uncomfortable until you are used to that vibration, or perhaps you do not need that energy in your life at that precise moment in time. So if you've been wondering why some people instantly turn you on or off, the answer lies in the notes or energy vibrations of those around you.

Many people believe that changing their names can make them happier, healthier, wealthier, more sexually attractive, and in some way it can miraculously change their life. However, the best names for your soul growth are those you were given at birth – the names written in ink on your birth certificate. When you are at one with yourself and your true vibration you are making the most of your potential, and life supports you to achieve your goals. The vibration of your Date Of Birth blends with your name vibrations and together they play an important role; they work together to harmonize your past, present and future potential. The blending of all the sound vibrations in your overall birth chart offers unique experiences so that you can express who you truly are and explore each area of your life fully.

Names influence your life in many different ways. The First Name offers you insights into your spiritual aspirations and personal goals. Middle Names are your personal support team that provide you with extra resources; qualities you can rely upon during times of crisis or spiritual growth. Some people use their Middle Name as a First Name but this may imply a desire to avoid certain experiences or lessons contained within the First Name (consciously or subconsciously). It takes courage to change, but using your First Name as a first name can open the store cupboard and maximize your true potential.

The Family Name (Surname) brings powerful karmic lessons or important issues for your family to work on together; lessons from your genetic family tree that may have been explored for generations. For example, Family Name Number 6 carries the potential for service, duty, creativity, compassion, selfishness, obsession and neglect. One family member is a doctor (service and compassion), another member is a model who neglects family gatherings (love of glamour, selfishness), and the next member is an interior designer (creativity). Every family member in your family group is working to balance the qualities of their Family Name Number. The family group can turn around patterns of behaviour and heal family issues from past generations. Indeed it provides wonderful opportunities to put the past to rest.

The overall sound vibration from your full birth names is called The Expression Number and offers you gifts and wisdom from all the experiences you have been through in the past (or past lives). What an incredible pool to be able to delve into, and to become familiar with its qualities so that you can utilize this potential within every area of your life.

Life is a journey, but the soul goes on many excursions when you sleep at night and over many lifetimes. One way of looking at the full birth names is to see the first letter or number of the First Name as the soul number influencing the beginning of the baby's life and the last letter of the Family Name influencing the end of life. If you believe in past lives you may see the first letter as a representation of the lessons being worked through at the ending of the baby's previous life. Similarly, you may see the last letter of the full birth names as a representation of the baby's maximum soul potential for this lifetime and for rebirth in the next. (These letters or vibrations also interplay with the date of birth, and it's the overall birth chart including birth names that ultimately governs the soul experience.) All the other letters in between the first and last letters of the full birth names represent the process in between birth and death: life lessons, qualities, karma and hidden potential. Indeed, in the present you always need to take into account where you've been in the past and soul potential for the future in order to attain a true picture of your life. You can read information on each individual letter of the alphabet in Chapter 5, 'Name Changing'.

So how important are names and the words you use to name those around you? Incredibly potent! When you name a baby or a person, you are learning to take responsibility for yourself and also the world around you. It is a huge responsibility because the names you give out are repeated many times each day. Numerology is a fascinating tool that helps you to discover the exact messages of the sounds, names or words you are projecting out into the world, and it enables you to recognize the truth. Name vibrations influence the environment and all the experiences your baby will have throughout life.

The process of naming your child, someone or something, helps to make it real – you can suddenly touch it, feel it and see it. Names allow you to look at qualities or issues objectively, which enables you to gain great insights and clarity. Life is a mirroring process and what you experience in your external environment are all aspects of yourself waiting to be recognized and healed; at a soul level we are all one. Experiencing different name vibrations (children, partner, family, friends, etc.) can help you to recognize what life's about, and help you to rise in consciousness. Humanity is constantly working to harmonize all the beautiful names or notes together, and everyone plays a part.

You and your baby's names or energy vibrations exactly match the qualities and potential needed for soul growth and they are divinely perfect. Therefore, relax when naming your baby and enjoy the mixture of nerves and excitement. It can be tricky if you feel pressurized to name your baby by grand-parents' or other extended family member's names. Subconsciously, baby names are always taken on for the best of the whole family group, which explains why there is often so much interference (healing potential) from the family group. Rest assured, as you're making your choice the right names do materialize for your baby but Numerology can guide you with those all-important clues.

Looking at names in terms of soul growth, the majority of a baby's karmic lessons in life are derived from either the maternal or paternal side of the genetic family tree (a professional Numerologist can help you to identify which side may be influencing your baby the most). For example, physically you look more like your father's side of the family, whilst your intellectual capabilities are more from your mother's side. You obtained DNA from both parents, so they were able to obtain clues for your birth names by looking at the numbers in their own birth charts. This enabled them to see which characteristics and vibrations they felt they shared with you as a baby, in order to help them make the best choice of name. Perhaps they also noted the significance of the Missing Numbers in their charts (see Chapter 5 'Name Changing'), or looked at their Personal Year Numbers to see if those numbers were relevant for you.

So your baby's names are for life, right? Yes, because the influence of the birth names always remains present in the background even if they are changed later on in life. Also, no, because some people are never happy with their lot in life and what they have been divinely given. Ideally, it's important to look at why you feel uncomfortable with your names, and what you don't like. This can provide incredible insights and help you and your children to heal the past (and your family tree). You may be able to recognize and learn important issues and lessons associated with your birth name vibrations. This can ultimately help to increase your potential for balance and harmony in your life, and therefore help to influence the world in a positive way.

However, if you or your baby truly desire a name change then Numerology is the tool for you; it can help you to explore your married name or to find a great Stage Name, and it can enlighten you on pseudonyms. Taking on new name vibrations helps to bring out qualities from within your overall birth chart. But if the new names don't fit, then life may become hard work or leave you feeling confused and wondering just what is going on. So it's important to use your intuition, and to choose new names carefully.

Numerology can help you to discover why your boss, lover or friend calls you by a specific Pet Name or Pseudonym, and it can indicate what they may really think of you, what they may want or need from you, and how they may want to relate to you (and vice versa). It also helps to highlight what levels you may be working on together – physical, emotional, mental or spiritual. For example, Jonathan's mother calls him by his full names (adds up to 2); she sees him as a sensitive soul and feels an emotional bond with him. His bank manager calls him Johnny (adds up to 5); communication is important in their relationship. Jonathan's lover (Samantha) calls him Jon (adds up to 3), indicating that she may want him to be fun, expressive or tactile and also that she may be a little judgemental too. It's fascinating to work out the numerology of Pet Names as they can offer vital clues to the true nature of all your relationships.

This book can help you to explore many different types of name vibrations with your eyes open. You can discover clues about potential: behaviour, characteristics, soul work, and also major personal and family karmic lessons. It can help you to tap into each unique spiritual blueprint so that your baby can receive the best possible names for their growth. Throughout the book each name description offers the essence or true potential of that name, but your baby (and you) may not utilize or explore every single aspect of that name. Numerology is fascinating and fun and it will lead you on an incredible journey that will help you and your baby to feel more confident in your own skin, so that you can feel free to be yourself. Numerology helps you to connect with your soul, and to feel the common thread of love that bonds humanity together, and it can help your baby's soul to sing.

Chapter 2

# History

Pythagoras was a well-respected mathematician and philosopher who lived in Greece and Italy around 600BC. Much of modern-day Numerology is attributed to him and his teachings were profound. However, every culture has its own system of Numerology and applies it in different ways which reflect the consciousness of its people. But all systems meet in the centre, in the soul, and essentially speak the same language of truth. This book is based upon Esoteric Numerology, which focuses on the energy behind the numbers, and in doing so provides a bird's-eye view of names and numbers.

Numerology is a psychology, a philosophy and a science, and whether you are focusing on your physical body or your soul, it invites you to open up, to learn, to experience more of life, and to live up to your potential. It's an incredible tool that has the power to transform lives if used wisely. Time is counted in cycles, and history repeats itself until mistakes are recognized; finally lessons are learned which create happier, healthier and successful human beings, and also a more harmonious planet. Names help you to work through personal and collective karma (issues or lessons). Indeed, you can learn so much about characters throughout history by simply applying Numerology to their names; it may even change your outlook on world history or of the people who've shaped humanity into what it is today.

So when did humanity first notice numbers? When it noticed shapes. If you look at all the shapes around you, you will notice that they are all based upon circles and lines. In Sacred Geometry these shapes can be counted and measured to define its number. For example, a square has 4 sides and so its shape represents the number 4; earth, ground, structure, survival, responsibility. Everything within your environment is constantly talking to you, giving you clues and messages about its purpose or use. However, shapes are only there so you can connect with the subconscious soul intelligence behind them, and this is what's important. If you were simply to look at a shape you would get stuck in the physical world and life would remain the same because there would be no ability to change. It's only by bringing in the light of soul consciousness or potential that you are able to create new things or take on new attitudes in order to experience growth in any area of your life.

Humanity is constantly evolving, but if we had only looked to the past for answers to modern-day problems we would have been extinct by now. For example, what use would a hand-held camping compass be for flying an aeroplane today when it requires sophisticated electronics to function correctly, or what use would chalk, rocks or sticks be when you need to be able to write on a computer? But we can find clues from the past and then apply soul intelligence and intuition in order to guide us towards a better future. Humans are always pushing the boundaries, which is why now, only 45 or so years after Man first landed on the moon, they are planning tourist trips into space. So it's soul potential that we're after; by tapping into the subconscious energy behind names and numbers we can discover infinite possibilities for personal and collective change.

In ancient times names were given generically. So, for example, if you lived in a tribe you would have been known by the name of that tribe rather than by an individual name. It was the same for many religions too. For example, in some religious orders you took on a new name so that your personal identity remained hidden and you could blend into the group. Being in a group meant that the religion or tribe kept its strength and provided more likelihood for its survival. However, religion has played and still does play an enormous role in the names that are given to babies, and names that are constantly at the top of popularity lists around the world today have remained the same for millennia. Many of these names are linked to old religious texts, or are names of Saints or Archangels. For example, Mary, Jack, Catherine, Mohammed, Joshua and Sara. However, whilst these names are socially recognized by religious groups, it's good to remember that even the most modern names like Apple or Peaches carry the same vibrations and the common seed, and are therefore of equal measure. Numerology links all languages and faiths together as one soul because we *are* all one.

## Generic Name, Cultural Example:

So let's explore the generic name Marie, which is commonly used in France to link with another name: Marie-Dominique, Marie-Françoise, Marie-Gabrielle. The names Marie, Maria and Mary may appear to be similar but they provide completely different potential as they're different number vibrations.

> **MARY**
> 4+1+9+7 = 21; 2+1 = 3. Mary = 3
> **MARIA**
> 4+1+9+9+1 = 24; 2+4 = 6. Maria = 6
> **MARIE**
> 4+1+9+9+5 = 28; 2+8 = 10; 1+0 = 1. Marie = 1

So the French culture is working strongly with the number 1 for its females. People with 1s tend to be leaders, pioneers, ambitious and headstrong, and they go for what they want. They also need to learn to explore their unique individuality, and find their own direction instead of looking to others to tell them what to do. So the idea of Marie is to give purpose, direction and originality (qualities of the number 1) to the other name number it's linked with, and then for this 1 energy to be blended together. For example, with the name Marie-Gabrielle, Marie = 1, Gabrielle = 8; 1 + 8 = 9. The final number 9 becomes Marie-Gabrielle's First Name Number as the two names are linked together as one (you also can also take into consideration the two individual name numbers if you choose).

# Classical and Traditional Meanings

The following names have been passed down through generations and can be found in every culture. You will have read up on baby names and seen classical and traditional translations next to each name. It's incredible to realize that they correspond with their Numerological translations; those who first chose these beautiful descriptions were wise indeed. Numerological translations offer great detail and provide an abundance of information for each name. Here are some examples of key similarities between both systems.

### LEYLA (f)
$3+5+7+3+1 = 19; 1+9 = 10; 1+0 = 1$

Leyla is a Turkish name and its classical translation is: Burn at Night.

The name Leyla adds up to a 19 overall and this is the number for the planet Sirius; the sun behind our sun that provides solar heat for all life to survive. Sun means soul and at night the physical body is rested so that the soul can be temporarily released to do its work. 19 adds up to a 1; let the purpose of your life be in line with the greater will of god (soul).

### DONALD (m)
$4+6+5+1+3+4 = 23; 2+3= 5$

Donald is a Celtic name and its classical translation is: Ruler of the World.

The name Donald adds up to 23 overall and this number represents the expansive mind or soul; learn to be ruled by your soul rather than your desire for sensory delights. 23 adds up to a 5; communicate with your soul and it will give you clarity about how to live a virtuous life.

### KANDA (f)
2+1+5+4+1 = 13; 1+3 = 4

Kanda is Native American and its classical translation is: Magical Power.

The name Kanda adds up to a 13 overall and in the past this number was linked with wise or Holy Men who were able to instigate change within their communities, and so were often looked upon as special. Number 13/4 represents great opportunities for change. So your lesson is to go for spiritual growth rather than staying stuck in a rut, so that you can enrich your life.

### ACE (m)
1+3+5 = 9

Ace is a Latin name and its classical translation is: Unity.

The name Ace adds up to a 9 and this number contains all the other numbers, 1 to 9, within it and so it represents humanity as one soul, along with the qualities of equality and inclusiveness. 9 is an expansive number as it sees everything and knows everything. So your lesson is to learn humility and share your knowledge with the world.

# Chapter 3

# How to Transcribe Names into Numbers and Draw Up a Birth Chart

When drawing up a Numerology Birth Chart for your baby (and for you!) it's good to be clear about what each area of your baby's chart represents. So, for example, the First Name Number relates to the first name, the Middle Name Number relates to one or more middle names, and the Family Name Number relates to the Surname. From these three names you can then work out The Expression Number, which represents the total of all the names on the birth certificate.

With Baby's Date of Birth you can then add more information by working out The Personality Number and The Life Path Number, and The Personal Year Number. Each number is important but all the numbers in the overall birth chart blend together and work with and through each other, and it's this blueprint that makes your baby's potential in life so unique.

Most mothers feel an instinctive sense about names for their unborn baby in the womb when there is a strong bond between the two, whilst others wait until the baby is born to see what the baby looks like or to be able to recognize characteristics the baby displays. However, if your baby has already been born then the Date of Birth offers an enormous amount of clues about what energy or names your baby may need.

Remember, the descriptions of each name provide clues as to the essence of the baby's soul and not all the qualities will be utilized by your child as the vibrations always contain far more potential than can ever be used. Learn to read between the lines and trust your intuition because you know what's best for your baby.

## How to Transcribe Any Name into a Number Vibration

Look up each letter in the Alphabet Chart on page 19. Next add up the numbers in each name on the birth certificate individually. Finally add all the name numbers together. See the example below: Alexander Jake Peter Edwards.

# Alphabet Chart

| A | B | C | D | E | F | G | H | I |
|---|---|---|---|---|---|---|---|---|
| J | K | L | M | N | O | P | Q | R |
| S | T | U | V | W | X | Y | Z | |
| **1** | **2** | **3** | **4** | **5** | **6** | **7** | **8** | **9** |

NB: You may notice that some numbers add up to 11, 22, 33, where the single number is doubled. These are called Master or Mirror Numbers and can provide your baby with opportunities to serve humanity in some way. Keep adding these numbers together until they reach a single digit between 1 and 9. For example, 11; 1+1 = 2. However, the single numbers 1 to 9 are always the most potent and therefore the most important vibrations to focus upon when naming your baby.

### First Name

#### ALEXANDER

1+3+5+6+1+5+4+5+9 = 39; 3+9 = 12; 1+2 = 3. First Name Number is 3.

This name provides you with your personal goals and intentions, and gives you clues as to your desires in life.

### Middle Names

#### JAKE

1+1+2+5 = 9. Middle Name Number is 9.

#### PETER

7+5+2+5+9 = 18; 2+8 = 10; 1+0 = 1. Middle Name Number is 1.

These middle names provide you with your own personal support team; qualities and gifts you can utilize to help you attain personal goals and fulfil your intentions in life.

## Family Name

### EDWARDS

5+4+5+1+9+4+1 = 29; 2+9 = 11; 1+1 = 2. Surname or Family Name Number is a 2.

This name brings gifts, challenges and potential from the genetic family tree, with issues to resolve and strengths to be gained. If you have a double-barrelled name like Smith-Robertson, then you add up the individual names and take those into consideration, but it's the number created by joining the two names that carries the most weight.

## The Expression Number

### ALEXANDER JAKE PETER EDWARDS

Alexander (3), Jake (9), Peter (1), Edwards (2) =
3+9+1+2 = 15; 1+5 = 6. The Expression Number is a 6.

This represents the wisdom you've gained in the past (or past lives), and highlights ways in which you can ground this potential; health and lifestyle, career, relationships, and soul growth.

## How to Work Out Your Date of Birth, Personal Year Number, and a General Date

Now you can work out other areas of your Numerology Birth Chart.

*The Personality Number:* The Personality Numbers governs behaviour, psychological patterns, childhood conditioning. Add up all the numbers in the DAY of birth (i.e. 1st–31st).

> **Example: Date of Birth 6th November 2010 or 6.11.2010**
> The Personality Number is 6.

*The Life Path Number:* The Life Path Number governs your bigger purpose or direction in life, your soul work, and offers you a deeper meaning to life. Add up all the numbers in the DATE of birth.

> **Example: 6.11.2010 = 6+11+2+0+1+0 = 20; 2+0 = 2.**
> The Life Path Number is 2.

*The Personal Year Number:* The PYN changes each year from one birthday to the next. It helps you to explore qualities from your overall birth chart, and offers you a broader range of experiences. When your PYN is the same as one of the main numbers in your Birth Chart then it magnifies your potential, and it may be a very significant year. Add up the full DATE of your last birthday.

> **So if your last birthday was 6.11.2010, add**
> **6+11+2+0+1+0 = 20; 2+0 = 2.**
> Your Personal Year Number (PYN) is a 2.

# Key Trends for the Personal Year Numbers (PYN) 1 to 9

PYN 1: Follow own direction. Purpose.

PYN 2: Apply inner wisdom. Balance.

PYN 3: Expansion. Creativity.

PYN 4: Personal Responsibility. Survival.

PYN 5: Communication. Freedom.

PYN 6: Service. Love. Big picture.

PYN 7: Trust. Truth.

PYN 8: Responsibilities. Revaluation. Success.

PYN 9: Transformation. Power.

A *General or World Date*: add up all the numbers in the DATE.

**Example: 25th January 2012 or 25.1.2012.**

Add 25; 2+5 = 7 (the Day) and also add
25+1+2+0+1+2 = 31; 3+1 = 4 (the Date).
The World Date is influenced by the 7 and the 4.
The Day Number gives the details. Read Number 7
in 'Key Trends For World Dates' below.
The Date Number gives the deeper soul potential.
Read Number 4 in the 'Key Trends' in the PYNs
above.

# Key Trends for the General or World Date Numbers 1 to 9

1. The beginning of a journey. Intentions. Focus.

2. Openness. Decision-making.

3. Letting go. Observation.

4. Grounding. Going back to basics.

5. Experimentation. Exploration. Change.

6. Family. Community. Relationships.

7. Motivation. Manifestation. Nature.

8. Responsibilities. Success. Strength.

9. Transition. Allow and permit life to unfold.

Chapter 4

# Names Decoded

## Introduction

**W**ord vibrations are incredibly potent so it's important to know what you're really saying when you repeat a name. Have you ever chanted a prayer, mantra or poem in another language that sounds romantic and interesting yet you haven't a clue what the words are about? So you're sending energy and messages out into the world blindly. However, as you can find a translation for a mantra and discover its true intent, this book will also guide you with insider information, so that you're clued up on baby names. It's essential to read between the lines and to use your intuition when choosing your baby's name, and to allow your subconscious mind to speak to you. Be inspired on your journey!

### How to Look Up a Number

In this chapter you will find 9 sections, each containing information for the different types of Name Numbers 1 to 9.

First read Chapter 3, 'How to Transcribe Names into Numbers and Draw Up a Birth Chart', so you can work out your (and your partner's) birth chart, plus your baby's date of birth if your precious one has already been born. This can give you clues as to the type of names and number vibrations you intuitively feel may be right for your baby.

Each section also contains a list of multicultural boys' and girls' names alongside some key goals for each Name Number.

- *First Name Numbers*. If, for example, you work out a First Name Number to be a 6, then read the information under the First Name Number 6 heading.
- *Middle Name Numbers*. If, for example, you work out a Middle Name Number to be a 4, then read the information under the Middle Name Number 4 heading.
- *Family Name Numbers*. If, for example, you work out your baby's Surname or Family Name Number to be a 9, then read the information under the Family Name Number 9 heading.
- *Expression Numbers*. If, for example, you work out your baby's Expression Number to be a 1, then read the information under the Expression Number 1 heading.
- *Pet Names and Pseudonym Name Numbers*. If you work out your baby's Pet Name to be an 8, then read the information under the Pet Names and Pseudonyms Number 8 heading.

# Name Number 1

| First Names for Girls: | First Names for Boys: |
|---|---|
| Agnes | Adam |
| Cindy | Dimitri |
| Clarissa | Edward |
| Emily | Elliot |
| Iman | Gordon |
| India | Imran |
| Isi | Joseph |
| Kate | Luca |
| Marie | Lucien |
| Natasha | Pablo |
| Salma | Peter |
| Stacey | Plato |
| Tessa | Saleem |
| Zara | Si |
| Zoe | |

**KEY GOALS:**

*Independence. Leadership. Self-reliance.*

## First Name Number 1

Your goal in life is to learn to prioritize because you have so many ideas and thoughts ticking over in your head about what you want to do every day. For example, you have a computer lesson booked, a session at the gym to attend, plus a new project to work on. Making lists for each area of your life is one of your tricks of the trade, and you can scarcely function without them. You're incredibly focused on your goals, and day and night can pass you by because you're simply so involved. However, at times you may exclude friends and family and excuse yourself from experiencing wonderful new opportunities, so you're learning to be supple with your agenda.

You can be shy and withdrawn, but this may be a tactic you employ when you just need space to think, and so you create this temporary self-imposed exile. You may find people try to drag you out of yourself or situations, but you're headstrong, and neither heaven nor earth can force you to move until you're ready and you're willing.

You're happiest when you're left alone to do things your way. For example, you're determined to teach yourself how to programme new software into your computer and you categorically refuse to listen to advice. However, you're learning to listen to reason because you're not always right and sometimes others do know what's best. You can be self-centred and foolishly think the world revolves around you; you're learning to think of others.

You're performance-led, and you relate to life through your successes. But you're learning to develop a sense of true self-worth, and to see your whole life experience as a valuable opportunity to learn – this is success. You may be a trendsetter (by intention or default), a stylish modern-day dynamo that avidly strives to make an impression upon others. You do succeed in creating an impact in life.

## Middle Names Number 1

You can learn to be your own best friend by practising positive thinking, especially at times when your mind wanders off and your actions become less constructive. For example, whilst ceaselessly revising for an exam you can teach yourself to stop thinking you'll never pass, and instead programme your internal computer with 'yes I can'. You may sometimes launch into wild and unexpected outbursts of anger because you need to channel your creative energies fully. You may also spend too much time 'in your head'. However, learning to direct your energy into positive activities, like exercise, can help to provide a welcome release for pent-up emotions. This can have a positive and profound influence over all areas of your life.

This name vibration is helping you to break down resistance to change, so that you can bring new energy into your life, breathe fresh mountain-top air, and learn to view life from a different perspective. Change takes time, but mental clarity can support you to break through. Once you're sure of your intentions and you feel directional your life may fast-forward quickly. You may sometimes find yourself overachieving at any given time. Your brilliant mind is a tool for inventiveness, innovation and opportunity, and you may use these skills to support your success, happiness and spiritual growth in life.

## Family Name Number 1

Over the generations your family has been working towards unification. Some members may be strong individuals and independent thinkers who dive fully into life, whilst others may be detached and aloof, and may even be loners. However, you all get on better when there's a common purpose to aspire to, for example, organizing a wedding where you can all make a contribution and experience working together as one. Your family group is learning to hold the vision for others to materialize their dreams and goals, and to feel proud of others' achievements as well as your own.

At times you place yourself or your family on a pedestal because you so value all the unique areas of expertise. But you're learning by experience that soul is the true hero or heroine in any life story, and your family karma is teaching you to follow this lead. Indeed, you may spend a lifetime searching for the spiritual light within, or for a father figure to give your life a sense of purpose or direction. At the end of the day you're all learning to grow up and to rely on yourselves to find your own way home.

For generations your family has been very frank and surrendered their opinions easily, which may have caused wars or conflicts. You're all learning to be direct, whilst remembering to switch on your radar so that you can detect whether it's appropriate to involve yourself in situations and when to speak. Your family members value originality, and they give off a scent of eccentricity, which can bring on a deluge of attention. You may feel superior, but it's grounding to learn that everyone has something unique and different to bring to the table. You can be naïve but this leads you to experience life as an open book (rather than with a closed mind), which can sometimes help your family unit to stick together.

## Expression Number 1

In the past (or past lives) you may have been boastful of your achievements and ignorant of others' need. Perhaps you were ruthless in the pursuit of your goals, and executed your desires with little regard for the outcome it would have on others' lives. Now you're learning to take account of your actions, and to stand up for others' rights. Indeed, you're a torchbearer who is able to lead your team to safety even across the narrowest ledge – onwards and upwards until you reach your destination. You've learned to be agile, and can see many obstacles far ahead. This gift of foresight helps you to make the most of your potential in all areas of your life.

Your soul gifts are that you're fearless and possess a pioneering spirit, and so you travel on incredible journeys throughout life. You courageously take on board whatever challenges are presented to you, sometimes setting yourself tasks to accomplish the impossible, and you often succeed. You're drawn to the world of the subconscious mind and soul, but you're ambitious and you need to conquer the material world too. You can be highly secretive, which is great if you're guarding state secrets, but alarming when loved ones are trying to get close to you. You're scared of close attachment and you recoil when people probe into your private life or try to get too close; you may busy yourself so as to avoid them next time around. However, you're learning to reveal more of your true self, to develop intimacy in your relationships, and to get deeply involved in life.

You're a natural leader, but under pressure you may feel lost and want others to tell you what to do (you then think this attitude is self-defeatist). You're learning to connect with your soul and follow the inner pulse; the light is always guiding you.

## Pet Names and Pseudonyms Number 1

People may call you by this Pet Name or Pseudonym Number because it can help you to be more assertive and to find your personal will or power so that you can make your mark in the world. Perhaps you've been a bit withdrawn and isolated recently, or you've been feeling as though you're not achieving a lot in life. This Pet Name can help you to focus on some goal-setting and then to go for life full on.

You may like this name because it's teaching you to draw on your own resources and rely on yourself. You may feel uncomfortable with this vibration if you're out of touch with yourself or want to evade facing situations. This is because it encourages you to become more self-conscious and therefore more aware of what you need to do in life. It can help you to make new starts, and pay attention to whether your boss, friend, lover or personal trainer calls you by this name because they may be giving you this message.

You may call someone a Pet Name or Pseudonym Number 1 because you wish they would be more directional, or you want them to be able to fix their own problems, or perhaps because you want them to play an important role in your life. Perhaps you see them as your 'knight in shining armour' or hero of the day. You may view them as pervasive because they can penetrate your mind and connect with your heart and soul. You may project this name vibration because you want them to inject more energy and vitality into your professional or personal relationships. This name can help someone to become their own person, and you may want them to become more independent, ambitious and involved in life.

# Name Number 2

| First Names for Girls: | First Names for Boys: |
|---|---|
| Akiko | Adrian |
| Ann | Christian |
| Bridget | Conor |
| Catherine | Dylan |
| Des'ree | Felix |
| Diana | John |
| Jade | Joshua |
| Margaret | Kamal |
| Marina | Max |
| Nadia | Naoko |
| Rachel | Nori |
| Sarah | Paulo |
| Susan | Omar |
| Violet | Oscar |
| Zita | Wicasa |

KEY GOALS:
*Emotional balance. Decision-making. Wisdom.*

## First Name Number 2

Your goal in life is to learn to make decisions. You may sit on the fence weighing up this and that, until sometimes it's too late and life makes the decision for you. You may be seemingly glad of this, but if you make the decisions yourself, you may experience a better outcome. Life is teaching you to grow up fast and take responsibility for yourself. Important decisions are challenging to make, but by flexing your decision-making muscles over small decisions, like what to wear each day, bigger decisions may come more easily. Indeed, successful business people are notorious for making fast and definite decisions that they stick to, and you may be inspired by this gift and follow suit.

You're gentle, kind and caring, but you're a sensitive soul who craves emotional stability. You tend to shut down emotionally at the slightest twitch or hint of rejection. You may become sulky, argumentative and defensive, but just a few cuddles and a little love soon bring you back to yourself. You may enjoy being mothered and love participating in female activities with friends. However, you're learning to nurture and reassure yourself, particularly at times when you feel most vulnerable.

You're a good listener and a wonderfully protective shoulder to cry on because you're so open and can see both points of view. For example, your friends have split up and they want you to take sides but you're solid in the middle; you find a way to stay true to both. You may be prone to accidents at times when you're being too dreamy and vacant. However, meditation or yoga can help to bring you back to yourself and ground you in the present moment. You can also learn to become aware of yourself and your environment.

## Middle Names Number 2

You can learn to become your own best friend by keeping life simple. For example, you need to study for an exam, but at the same time you want to go to a friend's party. You can manage to do both but it may mean spending less time on each activity, which can compromise your efforts and enjoyment. Perhaps you make a simple decision to do your studies and go to see your friend another time. You genuinely desire an easy life and sometimes it is only your emotions that make life feel so complex and complicated. You can support yourself by learning to feel what's real and what's not at times when you're calm and centred, and when you're feeling more placid.

This name vibration is teaching you to support yourself in the same way you do others. For example, as one of life's little helpers you're always helping friends, family, neighbours, and even strangers, but you find it difficult to give to yourself. You're learning to listen to your own needs and to respond with equal love and care. You can be a friend to yourself by being more tolerant towards your imperfections, and so you can feel more at home in your skin.

## Family Name Number 2

For generations your family group has been working towards emotional equilibrium. Perhaps you're generally calm and placid, but other family members are temperamental or emotionally unstable at times. You're all sensitive people and you're able (consciously or unconsciously) to tap into each other's deepest fears or hidden pains, and bring them to the surface. Whilst this can feel very traumatic, it can also instigate a healing crisis out of which much good can come. Indeed, if a family member has been cut off from their emotions it can help them to release emotional blocks, so they can lead a happier life. Sometimes your family are needy, clingy and emotionally dependent, and you're all learning to find peace within yourselves. The karma of this group is to bond together; emotional starvation isn't an option with so many caring and sensitive people around.

Your family may be naturally cautious people, but they're also intuitive and so they seem to be able to over-ride their fears and get on with life. At times you may all get sucked into inertia, but you're learning to work through your feelings so you can remain productive. Sometimes you fight like cat and dog, and whilst you may sometimes try to manipulate a situation to get a specific result or desired reaction, you are all gradually learning the art of compromise.

Your family are adepts at diffusing situations, which is one of your group's karmic gifts; underneath you do know how to keep the seas calm in a storm. You're all brilliant negotiators, and you may be found huddled together in a corner wheeling and dealing, and from an early age. However, you're learning to bandy a deal without asserting your emotions, which may prove challenging for your highly sensitive family members at times. Being 'plain and sane' may also help you to be successful in all areas of life.

## Expression Number 2

In the past (or past lives) you may have been a powerful silent leader. Perhaps you were the driving force behind important situations or behind people who went on to achieve great things; you made an incredible impact upon people's lives. Whilst you love supporting others, you're now learning to allow your soul to sing, your gifts to shine, and to take credit where it's due.

Your soul gifts are love and cooperation, and you've learned that joining forces with people is the fastest way to materialize dreams and to maintain a sense of equilibrium. Indeed, you're happy to share your workload and your last dime with those in need. In the past (or past lives) you may have been competitive, but you've learned to argue without emotion and to put across the collective point of view. You're generally diplomatic, because at heart you want to keep the peace and you do your best to ensure that situations remain healthy. You feel that love conquers all, and however tired or stressed you are, you aim to be more giving and to put yourself in others' shoes.

You're wonderfully receptive to new ideas, and your openness engages people in conversation. You welcome people warmly into your life and allow them to get close, particularly emotionally, and so they feel as though they can relate. Under pressure you may become emotionally fragile and oversensitive, and so you push people away by being overprotective. However, you're learning to use your inner wisdom to discover what's going on inside of you. You're searching for a soul mate so that you can walk through life with that special one. Indeed, you may feel incomplete without a partner or best friend by your side. However, you're learning to bond with your soul, and with the whole brotherhood of man, so you're actually spoilt for choice.

## Pet Names and Pseudonyms Number 2

People may call you by a Pet Name or Pseudonym Number 2 because it can help you to open up emotionally and be more reciprocative with them, or because they feel it can help you all to relate. In a work situation it may also help you, for example, to remain impartial to others' opinions so that you can make your own decisions and feel happy with them, whatever the outcome. You can't please everyone. Perhaps people feel this name can teach you to share more of yourself if you are someone who's generally quiet and shy, or if you hide away from the limelight.

You may like this name because it inspires you to use your gifts, and to feel emotionally secure within yourself. You may feel uncomfortable with this vibration if you feel like you're being hunted down in order to be responsive or make decisions, and you may not want to hear. However, it can help you to weigh up situations more carefully and to be more considerate towards others' feeling.

You may call someone a Pet Name or Pseudonym Number 2 because you want him or her to be calmer and less highly strung. Perhaps they may suffer from extreme emotions, which disturb their life and your peace. You may use this name at times when you want someone to pay close attention to what you're saying, and you feel like you really need to be heard.

You may use this name when you want someone to

compromise; perhaps you feel poles apart and you'd like to create a space where you can meet. You may also project this name because you want people to feel safe in your company (and vice versa), and to feel reassured that you're both there to support one another. You may like using this name because it makes you feel more loving towards this person or because it helps them be able to feel what you're about.

# Name Number 3

| First Names for Girls: | First Names for Boys: |
| --- | --- |
| Alice | Alexander |
| Claire | Amos |
| Eugenie | Austin |
| Farida | Charles |
| Frances | Duncan |
| Kai | Ethan |
| Lilian | George |
| Luna | Graham |
| Mary | James |
| May | Jermaine |
| Peaches | Joe |
| Ruby | Lennox |
| Rose | Madison |
| Sasha | Shui |
| Tandi | Tobias |

KEY GOALS:
*Creativity. Joy. Adaptability.*

## First Name Number 3

Your goal is to learn to take life in your stride, because sometimes you're easily thrown off track by trivial issues that wear you down. Perhaps you're great at multi-tasking and you achieve a lot in a day, but by adopting a more *laissez-faire* attitude you may achieve even more in your life. You're generally an optimistic person, but you can be your own worst enemy at times when you criticize yourself and pick on others. Indeed, you may feel happier within yourself if you accept that everyone's living and learning and allow people and situations to be.

You're fun-loving and gregarious, with a wicked sense of humour, but you can be fiery and wild at times; you may enjoy practical jokes but recognize when it's a good time to stop. You're learning how to play, how to live harmlessly, and also when to let things go. You may be an exhibitionist, which is great if you're on the stage or are an entertainer, but it may not always bring you the attention you want, or give you what you need. You're loving and affectionate and you welcome hugs and kisses any time of the day or night; you find it so uplifting. Indeed, giving to others is one way you can forget yourself.

You may be great at sports, entertaining, and making things with your hands, but you're learning to finish what you start so that you can become even more successful in all areas of your life. You can be scatter-brained at times, but your busy-bee lifestyle is no excuse for mistakes or lack; you're learning to get a grip on your situation by focusing on the here and now. Life is leading you on a journey and you're actively making the most of your opportunities.

## Middle Names Number 3

You can learn to become your own best friend by being more adaptable in life, instead of boiling over with frustration and feeling like there's nowhere to go. For example, your family are moving abroad, but you have lots of good friends nearby and you want to stay in your home. However, being more easy-going means you can welcome new pastures, new people and wonderful new experiences into your life.

This name can help to support you during times of anguish and pessimism, so that you learn to confront important issues rather than brushing them under the carpet. You may feel that you just can't be bothered or couldn't care less about a situation, but who are you fooling? This name can help you to move on from stuck situations by supporting you to learn from your mistakes and to take positive actions forwards.

When you're busy you may pick at food on the run from one appointment to the next. You can support your health and lifestyle by learning to relax, by eating the right foods, and by being kind to yourself. Perhaps you take up a hobby, like massage, art, hairdressing or cooking, which are absorbing and allow you to switch off and enjoy.

## Family Name Number 3

Over the generations your family has been learning about self-acceptance as individuals, and about how to accept each other within your group. For example, you may all possess strong beliefs about the way you 'should' conduct your personal lives, or about your religious or political points of view. You may criticize each other over your differences, pull each other down at any given opportunity, and generally give yourselves and each other a hard time. For generations you've been learning how to get along together so you can all be more relaxed and enjoy life.

Your family may have issues with social acceptance, and your group values society and wants to fit in. Perhaps your family possess outstanding social skills. You may spend time in very different social spheres, which may cause arguments and conflicts between you. However, you're learning to be tolerant to those from all social backgrounds and to accept people as they are. You're also learning to recognize that the world is one big melting pot and there's plenty of room for everyone, including your family members! Your family may be outgoing and feel confident in social situations, and enjoy discussing social issues because they are interested in people's welfare. They may possess strong opinions about what can be done to make life easier for society, and about ways to help keep life flowing and upbeat.

Your family karma may be that of abundance and prosperity, which may be due to earnings from all your various creative gifts. Indeed, you are able to uplift each other with your creativity. For example, you're inspired by your sister who's an artist (she encourages you to paint) and by your father who's a brilliant writer (you get to know him better through his words), whilst they're all impressed with your cooking! Your family are great at providing fun things to do on rainy days, and may enjoy backpacking around the world together, larking around and having a good time.

## Expression Number 3

In the past (or past lives) you may have been too carefree with your actions or words and it may have put others in danger, or you may have left a trail of destruction behind you. Perhaps when you were found out you even tried to divert attention away from yourself as you tried to squirm out of the mess you'd created. Now you're learning about consequences, and that you may find yourself in deep water if you avoid or forget to address situations. You're recognizing that you can only progress in life when each step along the journey is accounted for, and you're observing and learning how you can do better.

Your soul gift is that you are supremely self-confident. You're able to forget yourself and do what you're good at, and absorb yourself completely into life. You feel good about life, and people are drawn to your ease of manner because it uplifts them and helps them to relax. You may attract lots of friends and acquaintances and you can talk to anyone. However, you dislike gossip and you may resent others for repeating your conversations. But it serves a purpose because it gives people something to do, and keeps you and them busy by presenting you with issues to work through.

Under pressure your muscles may get tied in knots as you overwork, overplay and overdo things to the point of exhaustion. At these times you spread yourself too thin and rush off in different directions. You're learning to find stillness within (through meditation or quiet times) so that you can quieten your mind and harness your energy. You may also relax by playing sport (for fun rather than competition), and by maintaining your terrific sense of humour.

## Pet Names and Pseudonyms Number 3

People may call you by a Pet Name or Pseudonym Number 3 because they want to help you to be able to express yourself more fully in all areas of your life. Perhaps you find it difficult to let go and to express your feelings, or to dance and express the rhythm of your soul. Perhaps they call you this name because they want to get on down and PARTY and they know you're the expert and you can show them a good time.

You may like being called this name because it helps you to tackle your chores and gives you the energy to carry on until your shopping list is complete. You may feel more confident within yourself, or be more positive about life. You may feel uncomfortable if this name pulls you away from your situation in order to move you further along the road (and you don't want to budge). You're learning to go with the flow.

You may call people by this name because you want them to be more productive. For example, at home or work when there's a lot to do and you need a helping hand. Perhaps you really want people to have more sunshine and joy in their lives, and for them to be more optimistic and so uplift your environment.

You may use this name at times when you want people to be more loving and affectionate towards you. Perhaps you want to set someone free, or you simply want to be left alone for five minutes to make a cup of tea. You may use this name when you want the communication to flow more easily between you, or you want people to be more accepting of your beliefs. You may want people to take you more seriously, and for them to give you all of their attention.

# Name Number 4

| First Names for Girls: | First Names for Boys: |
|---|---|
| Annabel | Abdul |
| Bryany | Christopher |
| Daisy | David |
| Gabriella | Dexter |
| Joan | Dominic |
| Karen | Finlay |
| Katya | Jacob |
| Lily | Lemar |
| Linda | Louis |
| Lola | Luke |
| Maya | Rory |
| Paloma | Rudolph |
| Sita | Ryan |
| Sonia | Tejpaul |
| Tara | Thomas |

**KEY GOALS:**
*Responsibility. Endurance. Efficiency.*

## First Name Number 4

Your goal is to learn to apply yourself to life so that you can achieve your goals. For example, you may at times be lazy and actively allow or even encourage others to do your work for you. However, when you hold an attractive goal in mind, your determination drives you into action, and you plod through each step until you reach your destination. You're like a mountain goat that never gives up – let no one underestimate your capabilities!

You're incredibly practical. For example, your cat or dog has died and whilst you're heartbroken at losing your loyal friend you may be already looking through dog kennels. This bears no reflection on your ability to love but you feel lost without your routine. This applies to all areas of your life because change unsettles you, and you are always keen to settle into a new routine as soon as you can.

However, habits may become so ingrained that you find it near impossible to change, and you may find life delving deeper into dullness by the day. Sometimes it takes a very good friend to change in order for you to follow suit. 'I'm picking you up in my car at 8am and not 8.30 every day,' they exclaim, which may force you to adopt a new routine. However, if you are able to see that new suggestions can help your life to run more efficiently then you are prepared to make the effort and fall in line.

You're wonderful at creating life-long friendships because you stick with people through thick and thin. You're incredibly loyal and reliable, and are as solid as a rock during times of crisis. You may fight for friends' and family's rights and you may be passionate about their well-being and physical security.

## Middle Names Number 4

You're learning to be your own best friend by setting boundaries in your life. For example, by setting weekly times for socializing with friends, setting emotional boundaries by letting people know when there are issues you do not wish to discuss, and so on. Boundaries can help you to function physically, and like a security blanket they can support you to feel safe in life, particularly during times of change.

You may feel scared of the dark; perhaps there are aspects within yourself that feel like strangers to you too. You can support yourself to overcome your fear of the unknown by learning to face facts, and by learning to take life a day at a time so that situations become more manageable. You're methodical, and are able to conscientiously organize each area of your life into little compartments, but you can also support yourself to be even more productive by implementing a little self-discipline.

You like to spend your time constructively, and you want to make your mark on life. You may only truly feel satisfied when you are able to see tangible results from your efforts, and you may want to get noticed or want to be made to feel special. You're learning to acknowledge others' efforts and creative gifts too.

## Family Name Number 4

For generations your family has been working towards creating material security. This may include, on a biological level, the need to produce male heirs in order to secure growth of the financial pot so that inherited wealth stays within the family.

Perhaps you all argue over the many conditions and responsibilities that are endowed with owning property, land and possessions. Some family members may place far too much emphasis on material concerns, hoard money, or become mean, whilst others may be hopeless at managing their estate. Your group karma is to learn to take only what you need, so that everyone's needs are met. You're also learning to feel comfortable and secure within yourselves, so that you can walk through life unaided.

Over the generations your family may have been working on issues around responsibility. However, for some members the whole area of personal responsibility may simply not exist; they may fritter away money or fail to hold onto a respectable job. Whilst you may all want to provide a home or shelter for each other during times of crisis, you're learning that it's better to offer each other tools so that you can support yourselves, for example, by offering a job so that they have the ways and means to earn a living. Indeed, your family holds a very strong work ethic and this may over-ride any financial fragilities within your group.

Your family are incredibly hospitable and value family life, and are generally satisfied with their lot. You may be particularly drawn to exploring your family tree, to learn more about your ancestor's experiences, and to come to conclusions that may be of help to you and your family. You may also indulge in heraldry to discover more about your family's potential – gifts that may have been genetically passed down for you to use.

## Expression Number 4

In the past (or past lives) you may have found yourself fighting for survival, with each day presenting many more obstacles for you to overcome, just to stay alive. For example, perhaps you lived in the mountains of Tibet where you were forced to battle the elements, fend off bears, and live off a fundamental diet of yak's milk and butter all year through. Perhaps your hardships have left their mark on you, and you deeply resent it if you find yourself in a similar circumstance of lack. However, you may choose to regard all situations as character-building because they can actually help to make you stronger in the long run.

You may fear living or dying but you're learning to take full responsibility for yourself. Indeed, somewhere deep inside, you do know that you're one of life's survivors. You may store candles and torches in every room in case of an electrical power cut, and practically prepare yourself for every possible eventuality.

Under pressure you may be quick to make black-and-white decisions, which can have a dramatic effect upon your health, career and relationships. People may be surprised by your radical actions, especially if these lack integrity with the solid, stable character that you generally portray. You're learning to be more grounded during crises, and to view all situations as opportunities for spiritual growth and positive change. You may at times be a workaholic but you can feel torn apart by conflicts of responsibility. However, you're learning to compartmentalize different areas of your life, so there's room for everyone and everything.

Your soul gift is that you can provide structure for yourself and others, so that you can build a secure and comfortable life. You also possess endurance and stamina and altogether these can help to provide solid foundations for success in all areas of life.

## Pet Names and Pseudonyms Number 4

People may call you by a Pet Name or Pseudonym Number 4 because it can help you to be more dependable. Perhaps you're often late for appointments and you're now realizing how much this affects your own productivity and others' output when they're relying on you to get the job done. This name vibration can help you to be more practical and realistic about life, and it can help you to find the determination to carry on each day working towards your goals.

At times you may feel uncomfortable with this name because it takes you right back to basics and forces you to address all your personal responsibilities. However, you may enjoy this name because it makes you feel special and different or perhaps incredibly passionate too. If you've been 'sat on the fence' for ages dithering, this name can help you to grow up and live your life.

You may call someone a Pet Name or Pseudonym Number 4 because you want to feel more secure within your friendship and you're hoping this will bring you closer together. Perhaps you're looking for someone to take good care of you (practically and materially) and so you project this name onto others. You may use this name at times when you're feeling insecure and you need a friend.

You may call people this name at times when you want

them to take more practical care of themselves. For example, your mother's been eating all the wrong foods and putting on weight to boot; it may help her to take practical steps towards a healthier lifestyle. It may also help others to confront fundamental issues that have been keeping their needle stuck in the groove, so that they can progress in life. This name vibration can help people to embrace life a day at a time.

# Name Number 5

| First Names for Girls: | First Names for Boys: |
|---|---|
| Anya | Benjamin |
| Caitlin | Carlos |
| Caroline | Cyrus |
| Chantal | Davinder |
| Emma | Frank |
| Evie | Gregory |
| Fatima | Kent |
| Kimberly | Leo |
| Lisa | Lewis |
| Mirabelle | Malo |
| Molly | Morgan |
| Olivia | Paul |
| Samantha | Reed |
| Sophia | Rodrigo |
| Tamsin | Wayne |

KEY GOALS:

*Communication. Knowledge. Freedom.*

**First Name Number 5**

Your goal in life is to keep your mind occupied with new information because you crave stimulation. This may be on the mental level where you enjoy reading, studying and meeting new people, and also tennis or skiing, which require you to be mentally agile. Indeed you may be addicted to getting your daily adrenalin fix, possibly through using hard substances, alcohol, exercise, chocolate, work or even people (sexually), but you're fast learning the art of restraint. You're also learning common sense because you tend to jump into situations without thinking and land in the deep end. Living on the edge is only one way to keep your senses stimulated and your mind ticking. You may be a computer whizz, and you know exactly where to locate the information you need, but your joy comes when you are able to pass it on to others. Indeed, you're a natural at networking, and the social groups you belong to may rake in people by the millions because you know how to keep them fascinated.

You enjoy experimentation and your natural curiosity leads you into interesting situations because you're adventurous too. Perhaps you want to be a space traveller and visit extraterrestrial locations – just for kicks – or learn how to master the Kama Sutra or how to be an expert at chess. You enjoy diversity but you're easily bored; you're learning to stick to your commitments. You may find it easier to commit if you carry out thorough research before saying, 'yes,' or 'I do.'

You're wonderful at talking to people, and you're overwhelmingly witty, perceptive, and observant – you study your subjects intently. You're extremely persuasive, and you mesmerize people with facts and figures. Yes, you ooze the 'X' factor. You're uninhibited and you love dancing and singing, but you adore discovering new scientific facts about life and the universe.

## Middle Names Number 5

You can learn to become your own best friend by being more spontaneous, so that you can ride out change. Life is continually shifting and moving, and even if you try to stay stuck it finds mysterious or surprising ways to shake things up and move you on. However, in order to change your circumstances you're learning to look at the reasons why and how you're experiencing the situation, and to identify all the key lessons involved. You may avidly look at details, and try to reason with yourself or demonstrate to others why things are the way they are. But, you're learning to observe life from the perspective of your soul; by taking a global view you can gain great insights and life suddenly makes sense.

This name vibration is teaching you to support yourself by being more reliable, because you're as changeable as the wind. You jump from one event to the next, or change your wardrobe continuously (which you love because it keeps people guessing). Perhaps you associate 'reliable' with 'boring', but at times you do need to stay still in order to take a breath and grow spiritually. You're easily excitable and your natural vivaciousness guarantees that you live life full on.

## Family Name Number 5

Over the generations your family group has been working towards honouring their commitments. Your family may feel a deep soul connection already, or perhaps some members feel trapped or smothered by your closeness, and want to get out. You may be a family of travellers who explore all four corners of the world, which is great as long as you're not running away from facing facts. Indeed, your family is learning to explore emotional ties, to help you all clear up past hurts and misunderstandings and get even closer. Healing your emotions may help you to make deeper commitments to each other, to yourself and to life.

Your family karma is to share your knowledge and to become a messenger of truth. Some of your family members may be naturally sceptical about anything new and seek out evidence as proof, and only then when something has been accepted as fact can it be passed on to others. Other members may endlessly speculate about life or over-analyse situations, which gets them nowhere. However, you're able to see situations from a scientific point of view, but it's soul awareness that brings you the most clarity.

For generations your family has studied or been interested in anthropology, and you may possess a good working knowledge of people or possess honed people skills. However, you may be suspicious of people at times, and like a private detective seek out clues to discover what's really going on behind closed doors. Your family possesses a general restlessness, and you may all leave no stone unturned as you jump from one lead to the next once you're following a scent. You're extremely pro-active, and if there are issues that need putting forward or information to correct, you'll all be there to push things through.

## Expression Number 5

In the past (or past lives) you may have been too quick to jump to conclusions about people or life, and it led you astray. For example, you may have been a science teacher who saw the light in your star pupils whilst dismissing others' opinions out of hand. So you were surprised and shocked when a student in the latter category went on to invent breakthrough technology. Now you're learning to pay attention to detail, and to notice what's going on so that you can gain clear insights into every situation. You're also learning to use your knowledge wisely and to divulge only what people need to know rather than deluging them with information.

Under pressure you may procrastinate or bury your head in the sand like an ostrich, but either way this restricts your situation even further. Freedom is important to you, and you may see problems – especially those that you can't instantly solve – as weights stopping you from progressing. However, you're learning to apply common sense because facing issues is your fastest route to freedom. Under pressure, you may also be drawn into addictions, but you're learning to explore the emptiness you feel so that you can gather strength and get back on track. You're learning to surround yourself with good friends and people with whom you can connect on your journey.

Your soul gift is communication, and you may speak many languages or work in the media. Perhaps you love writing various blogs on the internet, and enjoy lecturing others (in the literal or professional sense). You may be telepathic and receive and send instant messages, which saves time on calls and keeps life flowing. At times you can be extremely outspoken. This is a potent gift that you may consciously and harmlessly use, in order to shake up stale situations or bring people back to life. You offer them clarity so that they can see the light.

## Pet Names and Pseudonyms Number 5

People may call you by a Pet Name or Pseudonym Number 5 because it helps you to be more adventurous and to get more on top of life. This vibration can help you explore your sexuality. You may feel more attractive or find yourself telling loud lewd jokes that are so raunchy they could make Heidi Fleiss blush. This name vibration can also help you journey inwards towards your mind or soul to seek out knowledge and connect deeply with life.

You may like this name because it pumps you with vitality from your soul, which is the ultimate and infinite source of energy that provides you with constant stimulation in life. You may feel uncomfortable with this name if you're trying to avoid emotional intimacy; this name magnifies your sensitivity and so you may feel that situations are more intense. People may call you this name because they are in awe of your charisma or dazzled by your wit.

You may call people by a Pet Name or Pseudonym Number 5 if you want them to be more committed, which is particularly important if they are your business partner or lover. Perhaps you want them to open up and reveal more of their true self because you want to get closer but they're flitting around or travelling around all over the place. You may project this name onto a person whom you find sexually attractive when you're feeling hot and you're bursting to discover if you can make a special connection.

You may call someone by this name because you want them to release you from specific commitments, or because you want to help this person to release their own restrictions in life. You may call people this name when you feel they have their finger on the pulse, and you may want to join them in the fast lane too.

# Name Number 6

| First Names for Girls: | First Names for Boys: |
|---|---|
| Ava | Cameron |
| Cameron | Darcy |
| Camilla | Daryl |
| Christine | Fred |
| Claudine | Heath |
| Corinne | Ibrahim |
| Delilah | Jasper |
| Flavia | Kojo |
| Giselle | Lorenzo |
| Jemima | Michael |
| Maria | Patrick |
| Matilda | Rajiv |
| Millie | Robert |
| Sheree | Stephen |
| Suki | Vincent |

**KEY GOALS:**

*Harmony. Love. Service.*

## First Name Number 6

Your goal in life is to learn to see yourself as part of a family group, a soul group (humanity), and to recognize the gifts you bring to the team. For example, you may be great at football or hockey and play for your town or country, but each member brings individual skills to the team for it to function at its best. You're learning to focus on what you're good at, whilst continuing to love yourself at times when you miss your goals in life (or the team loses). Indeed, you may hold on to feelings of guilt, particularly if you know you've let someone down, or paradoxically you may project your guilt onto others by blaming them for your mistakes. You're learning to gather wisdom from all your experiences, so that your feelings remain intact and you learn to handle situations in a positive way.

You're loving and giving, and great at home-making; cooking, sewing, gardening and interior design may be your key interests in life. You fill your home with love and make it a place of warmth and welcome where others can take shelter and feel safe. You surround yourself with folk because you feel it's mutually beneficial. You love life's little luxuries and you pamper yourself with creature comforts because you feel you're worth it. At times you're spoilt rotten! You're learning that all the candies in the world cannot replace a hug with a loved one, a kiss, and those magical words – 'I love you.' Your bedroom may be filled with toys or dolls, and an abundance of photos of family and friends, along with animal memorabilia – you adore your furry friends.

You possess a strong sixth sense, and may experience psychic dreams or premonitions, but you're learning to take a step back from situations so that you can get life into perspective.

## Middle Names Number 6

You can learn to become your own best friend by going beyond the glamour of the image you see in the mirror and seeing the true reflection. For example, you're offered work on a project for a prestigious charity, which you love. However, once you're there you feel that all they want is to be seen to be doing something good, and perhaps they're not bothered about how much money they raise at all. However, you may offer the charity constructive criticism so they can improve upon their ethics, and provide a good service to their community. Similarly, you can help yourself to 'see things straight' at times when your emotions are running riot or you are viewing life through rose-coloured spectacles.

This name vibration can help support you to manage your timekeeping. You may constantly be late for appointments, or be so worried about being late that you turn up far too early. However, you're learning to monitor your movements so that you can make the most out of each day. Your soul has its own agenda, too. For example, you're going to watch a movie but the train turns up late and so you stay at home and perform essential duties, which are greatly needed and it works out for the best.

## Family Name Number 6

Over the generations your family have been learning to live and work together as a team. This is a celebration if you truly relish living in one another's pockets, but challenging if one of you wants space because duty calls 24/7. At times you may feel suffocated by the need to support family members, and you can all at times be emotionally needy. You may feel resentful at all the family gatherings, but you do throw yourselves into the events because you do what's best. Your family are like a swarm of insects swirling around together, and people hear the sound of the music you make from miles away. Indeed, others can tangibly feel the laughter, joy and the mutual support and connection between you, and they may find it uplifting. You're learning to value quality time spent in family union and also to see family life as sacrosanct. Indeed, the marriage vow, 'to love, honour and obey', may provide a beacon of hope for your family group. You can gather strength in the bosom of family life so that you can enter the big wide world with more love to give others.

For generations your family may have been selfish and neglected children or family responsibilities in exchange for satisfying their own selfish desires. However, there are always black sheep and nobody's perfect. Indeed, some family members may do everything in their power to preserve the unity and keep everyone together. For example, by working late into the night to earn a living that keeps a roof over your family's head. You may go far out of your way to make sure that all your family are safe, but like a pack of wild animals your family may seek revenge on anyone who dares to hurt one of your brood. However, your family karma is to learn to fend for yourselves and find your own way in life.

## Expression Number 6

In the past (or past lives) you may have been physically or emotionally abusive and inflicted great pain and suffering upon others. For example, perhaps you were a doctor who failed to keep needles clean or who gave operations without anaesthetic; perhaps you even enjoyed hurting others. Now you're learning to heal your own deep emotional scars and to love and respect yourself, so that then you really want to take good care of others. Indeed, deep down you dream of living a harmonious life and you may also want this for everyone. You tend to neglect your own needs and put others first, but you're gradually learning to bring yourself into the equation.

You enjoy eating healthy foods from the very best sources you can find, but under pressure your diet may take a bashing and comfort eating jumps to the rescue. You may obsessively overeat or alternatively neglect to feed yourself appropriately; you're learning to nurture yourself in order to be able to carry on at full capacity. Under pressure you may become bitter and resentful towards others, but you're learning to respect the choices you've made and that others are making in life.

Your soul gift is generosity, which people find endearing; you're likely to sacrifice your own desires in order to help the team. Sometimes you're self-indulgent emotionally, but that's a sin you can live with as long as you are able to continue to be of good use to others. You're a reasonable person, obliging and kind, but you're learning to say 'no' to people who take advantage of your good nature. You're highly creative, and you love the theatre, arts, and attending cultural events where you can feel connected to the rich diversity in life. You're pure love in action, and are happy to take on big commitments if it can support others' growth.

## Pet Names and Pseudonyms Number 6

People may call you by a Pet Name or Pseudonym Number 6 because it helps you to feel a part of the family. For example, it's your first day at school and this name helps you to feel welcome. It may also help you to bond with others emotionally, which is great if you want to get closer to family and friends. This name can bring out compassion, and help you to empathize with others so you can provide comfort where you can.

You may feel uncomfortable with this name because it may enable you to notice how jealous you can be of other people's gifts or attributes. This name can help to bring deep emotions to the surface when it's time for them to be released. This can help you to feel comfortable within yourself and happier with your lot in life. You may like this name because it makes you feel warm and tingly all over, or because it encourages you to fall in love with life over and over again.

You may call people a Pet Name or Pseudonym Number 6 when you want to turn a situation around to suit your own needs. Your sixth sense makes you feel that people may be able to deliver exactly what you want – chocolate cake, a wedding ring, or promotion – but feelings aren't always right. You may feel people are too self-obsessed and you want to take them out of themselves by demanding some of their valuable time and attention. Perhaps you feel people need to learn to be more respectful and considerate towards others (or you) and this name may help them to address these issues.

You may use this name when you want people to take more care over their physical appearance. Perhaps you may see this slackness as a marker that your relationship has slipped into complacency. However, this name can help you to connect through your heart because at the end of the day it's love that really counts. This name can bring out the angel or devil in people, so be prepared to see or visit extremes; 'all roads lead to Rome' and it can eventually lead to harmony.

# Name Number 7

| First Names for Girls: | First Names for Boys: |
|---|---|
| Anne | Anselmo |
| Berenice | Brad |
| Carolyn | Carl |
| Dakota | Chin |
| Elizabeth | Harry |
| Elle | Hasan |
| Francesca | Henry |
| Grace | Jack |
| Isabella | Giles |
| Lucy | Kevin |
| Osha | Miyoko |
| Stephanie | Neville |
| Susannah | Raphael |
| Victoria | Vladimir |
| Yvette | William |

**KEY GOALS:**

*Trust. Honesty. Introspection.*

## First Name Number 7

Your goal in life is to learn to become more sensitive to others' feelings and needs, because you can be extremely self-centred. Indeed, this may be unintentional as you often feel the need to close your shutters and withdraw from the world, and then you lose track of events and situations. You spend a lot of time wrapped up in your own little world, but instead of isolating yourself and alienating others you're learning to join the party. You have a strong presence and people sense this, but at times when you retreat into your imagination people find you vague, dreamy and unavailable. You're learning to ground yourself by being aware of everything you're doing and being present in the moment. You're a nature lover at heart and meditating (especially near trees), walking in the park and listening to gentle music may also help to bring you back to your senses.

You're intuitive and sometimes you may literally be 'away with the faeries', talking to your spirit guides or to angelic keepers. You're a natural healer and you have the ability to 'see right through' people, which is a wonderful gift that you're learning to use when required. You're like a wise old sage and may appear older than your years. You can be brutally honest but only those who want the truth listen to you; those who prefer to remain in the dark may sometimes react dramatically to your views. Whilst you may fear being misunderstood, you're learning to follow your truth and accept that everyone's different.

You're a fast learner, but you can be impatient and emotionally demanding at times. You excel at materializing your goals because you're highly productive. Like a tightrope walker you're learning to hold your nerves steady when you're focusing on your goals and there are hazardous challenges ahead. Panic attacks may be a sign that you need to learn to generally keep calm whilst waiting for things to happen; you're learning to stop and smell the roses.

## Middle Names Number 7

You can learn to become your own best friend by allowing yourself to be vulnerable in order to let life in. This is because you tend to protect yourself from getting hurt emotionally, and so avoid putting yourself in new situations which you fear may damage your health, relationships or career. Indeed, at times you may suffer from hypochondria but you're learning to stop focusing on every little movement your body makes. Like a Jack Russell you may be snappy, or bite people's heads off at the slightest sneeze, but like Jack you do sense exactly whom you can trust. Being open can help you to achieve spiritual growth and success in life.

This name is teaching you to support yourself by organizing quiet times each week where you can create space to think and where you can simply be. You may be interested in psychology because it helps you understand people and situations. Reading, writing a journal, or reflecting on (past) situations can help you gain deeper insights into how you can make the most of your journey. The solitude also helps you to recharge your batteries by plugging you back into the source or soul.

## Family Name Number 7

Over the generations your family have been working closely at the spiritual level to synthesize their union, therefore to raise the vibrations of the group. For example, some family members may be investment bankers who use their intuition to help them make instant decisions when trading currencies and commodities around the world. They may appear cold or materialistic when they may well be deeply connected to their spirituality or truth. Another member may be a holy person who travels consciously on the road to self-discovery or towards their Holy Grail. Your family karma is to learn to fuse all your many talents into one, and make one big beautiful rainbow together. At times you may feel like you don't belong, or fit into this family group, but this may be because you are isolating yourself or wanting to feel special. You're learning to appreciate one another and the amazing gifts you each bring to life.

For generations your family have been learning to be more transparent. You're all very sensitive and you can feel when something's not quite right or when there's been an evasion of truth. You're learning to be honest with yourselves so that you can become more productive as a group. You may value privacy, but when hidden secrets are discovered they may rock your reality and take family members some time to recover. However, the very process of discovering truth and trust can help to refine your family's spiritual connection and ultimately bring you closer together.

Your family may be movers and shakers who actively instigate change and are able to turn dreams into reality. Sometimes you may act like royalty. Perhaps you're incredibly fussy about what you eat, the way you look, and particular about the company you keep. Your family possess good manners but sometimes situations do require you to get your hands dirty in everyday life. You all possess a refined taste and enjoy fine wines, fine art, antiques, classical music, and a peaceful life.

## Expression Number 7

In the past (or past lives) you may have been used as a scapegoat for others' mistakes and misdemeanours. For example, you were a philosopher who believed the earth was round at a time when most believed it was flat. During an uprising of new public opinion you were targeted as a scapegoat for all those spreading this belief, and you were banished from the land. Perhaps you suffered a deep sense of betrayal because you had only told one 'friend' whom you felt you could trust. Now you're learning to trust yourself and to speak your truth regardless of whether others feel you're making up stories. You're learning to walk your talk and stand strong.

Under pressure you may withdraw into yourself and literally hide away from the world for days or even months, until you feel safe to face the music. By this time the storm may have passed, but so have opportunities. Under pressure you may take things too personally because you tend to be so centred on yourself. You're learning to be open and honest with others during an event rather than afterwards, so that it can help heal situations quicker and allow you all to move on.

Your soul gift is your intuition, and you're wonderful at exposing the truth and breaking down illusion, because you're able to view life from the soul perspective. Indeed, you may want to heal the world, and to see life progress positively. You're interested in philosophy, psychology and spirituality and you do your bit to preserve the environment. You're extremely health conscious, and you may practise tai chi, chi gong, meditation and eat a highly nutritious diet; you prefer to consume organic foods and water from pure sources. In the past (or past lives) you may have been very naïve, so now you're getting clued up on facts and facing reality.

## Pet Names and Pseudonyms Number 7

People may call you by a Pet Name or Pseudonym Number 7 because you're always trying to be one step ahead of the game, and it can help you to pace yourself, to be less anxious and more patient with life. This name vibration may help you to be more aware of the natural cycles that govern life (the seasons, day and night, life and death), so that you can observe and allow seeds to grow and blossom in their own time. This name may help to enhance your personal development or give your soul space to heal.

You may feel uncomfortable with this name if you're trying to protect yourself because it makes you feel exposed. Perhaps you want to remain distant whilst others want to access the real you, but this name can help you to connect with others. You may like this name because it helps you to be resourceful and to discover the ways and means of materializing your goals from deep within yourself. It may help you to get going.

You may call people a Pet Name or Pseudonym Number 7 because you truly feel they are kindred spirits, or because you enjoy a deep spiritual connection. Perhaps they are dreamy and unrealistic at times and you want to help them get a grip on reality. You may see them struggling with their identity and subconsciously feel this name can help put them 'straight' about who they really are. This person may be a great mirror for you to see yourself clearly if you're prepared to be honest with yourself about what you see (and vice versa).

You may use this name when you want people to show you appreciation, perhaps because you feel your efforts have been taken for granted recently. You may project this name because you want others to hold the fort and keep everyone together, or perhaps because you see them as playing a pivotal role in your life.

# Name Number 8

| First Names for Girls: | First Names for Boys: |
| --- | --- |
| Alexandra | Angus |
| Cassandra | Callum |
| Chantelle | Delmar |
| Cheryl | Guillaume |
| Fleur | Guy |
| Georgia | Hugh |
| Helen | Kyle |
| Jasmine | Liam |
| Lauren | Mason |
| Leah | Rupert |
| Octavia | Samuel |
| Olga | Spencer |
| Pia | Stefano |
| Zhen | Tyler |

**KEY GOALS:**
*Responsibility. Empowerment. Success.*

## First Name Number 8

Your goal is to be successful in all areas of life. If this means that you need to regularly train in new skills, attend personal or professional development courses, or meditate for inner wisdom and guidance, you're onto it. You're a shrewd cookie, and as with playing a game of chess you do recognize exactly what moves you need to make in order to achieve your goals. Success whets your appetite and leaves you wanting more; you may aggressively pursue bigger and more challenging goals and you mow down any obstacles blocking your target. Sometimes you can be materialistic and success feels empty, but you're learning to find inner satisfaction in everyday life. This process may lead you to go on spiritual journeys inwards to your soul, or outwards to attend spiritual or meditation retreats, to visit places of worship or to go on spa holidays, which cater for your mind, body and spirit.

You're great at being assertive and you can generally take care of your own affairs and fight your own battles. You may at times consciously allow people to control or direct you, simply because you like the idea of someone being able to give you direction. You may enjoy being submissive and for a short while you like it. You're strong willed and you may grate with those in authority, and you're a bossy boots who always want to be on top. You exude power and charm, and people may fall over themselves vying for your attention, which only massages your glowing ego. However, pride comes before a fall and you're learn-ing to be humble and to recognize there's light in everybody.

You possess a sophisticated taste. You may enjoy the smartest clothes, the most expensive jewellery, the trendiest music, and you may seek out a cosmopolitan lifestyle too.

## Middle Names Number 8

You can learn to become your own best friend by being more conscientious and organized, which can support you to be successful in every area of life. For example, if you organize your work, social and personal diaries well, you may also feel a great sense of satisfaction from your accomplishments. What you put in you get out, as you may have already learned through trial and error.

This name can support you in re-evaluating your life regularly, so that you avoid slipping into rigid patterns of behaviour or routines that may hold you back. If you feel that sometimes your life is spinning out of control it may help you to become more assertive, to boldly grab the steering wheel and take charge of your own destiny.

You can learn to support yourself by tapping into your inner strength during times of crisis, so that instead of looking for someone to lean on you can support yourself. Indeed, this inner strength empowers all areas of your life. At times your shoulders may feel heavy with burdens but you can learn to delegate responsibilities to help lighten your load. You can also support yourself by taking life and yourself less seriously.

## Family Name Number 8

For generations your family have been working to resolve power struggles within your group. Perhaps you've been waging war with each other continually over who controls the family business and the financial pot. Some members may crave the status of power (e.g. being the chairman of a prestigious company), whilst other members may crave money alone. Perhaps you want to disown the lot and calmly walk away from your inheritance. This may be because you know you can provide for yourself or because you have far too much pride to take money from your family. However, you're all budding entrepreneurs and so you may resolve to each take on an area of expertise for the family to function successfully, and to appease the genetic storms.

You may be a powerful family who excel at business, but you can all be prone to delusions of grandeur at times. You may feel threatened by families of equal status or by those who are even richer than you – perhaps you think you're truly indomitable. Your family may be ruthlessly competitive and at times hold on tightly to the power, status and authority you've inherited or created. However, you're all learning to surrender to situations that are out of your control and to do what's best. You can then gain all the inner strength you need to direct your family affairs with renewed purpose and integrity. You're all learning that whilst you can influence your fate, it's karma that ultimately seals the deal and delivers your daily dues according to the higher spiritual law of justice.

Your family may at times feel like slaves because you all work so hard at life. Some of you may be slaves to money, and other members may be slaves to soul. However, your family karma is teaching you all to find a healthy balance between spirit and matter so that you can live in harmony with the world and feel at peace with life.

## Expression Number 8

In the past (or past lives) you may have been greedy and possessive, and you may have regarded taking all that you want as your divine right, with little thought of others. For example, perhaps you were a landowner who paid your staff very little whilst dictating that they worked from dawn to dusk. You may have taken ownership of their homes and sold them off to make a profit, and then kept your staff holed up in abject poverty. Now you want to create win–win situations in all areas of your life, and you're learning to help people step onto the ladder of success. Perhaps you're only too eager to share your work and your worth with others. In your book everyone's a winner, and you're learning to celebrate others' achievements, even if they appear grander than your own.

Under pressure you may dig deep into a controlling mode in order to survive. Perhaps you become stubborn, non-cooperative or immovable in your opinions, which brings situations to a stalemate. You're learning to climb down from your castle so that you don't sabotage your life – everyone has issues to deal with and you're learning to grow up. At times you may experience graphic flashbacks to previous lives, or to situations in the past. Unfinished business always rears its head when you least expect it, and so you're learning to face situations and work through important issues.

Your soul gift is your inner strength, and you are a guide for others. You may also put your friends and family through trials and test their strength. You may present people with tough lessons; these can ultimately help to make you all stronger in spirit and help you to lead more fulfilled and successful lives.

## Pet Names and Pseudonyms Number 8

People may call you by a Pet Name or Pseudonym Number 8 because it helps you be more assertive or feel more seductive. Perhaps it brings out the tiger in you and you change your dress code to something hot or sophisticated. If you're looking for promotion and want to make a good impression upon your boss or to charm the person of your dreams, this name may be a tower of strength. However, you always attract what is divinely yours. Others may call you by this name because they want to boost your ego, or because they look up to you.

You may feel uncomfortable with this name if you find yourself being too structured or rigid because you're a free spirit. You may like this name because it helps you to address important issues and wakes you up to your spirituality.

You may call people by a Pet Name or Pseudonym Number 8 because you want them to be your 'knight in shining armour' or because you need their guidance. Perhaps you are at a crossroads in life. You may possess a karmic connection with this person and you may be teaching each other major lessons in life. Indeed, this person may turn your life upside down so that you can see life from another perspective for a while. Perhaps you see this person as ostentatious, materialistic, or irresponsible, and you're hoping they will polish up their actions and their outlook on life, and get real.

You may use this name for those you see as successful in life. You may want others to stop intellectualizing and to get on and follow their ambitions. Perhaps you are seduced by people's power, possessions or expensive taste; you're all learning to find a deeper meaning to life.

# Name Number 9

| First Names for Girls: | First Names for Boys: |
| --- | --- |
| Augusta | Alfonse |
| Beatrice | Ashok |
| Carlotta | Boris |
| Charmaine | Daniel |
| Coco | Jake |
| Ha | Jay |
| Helena | Matthew |
| Jennifer | Mohammed |
| Judith | Nicholas |
| Mercedes | Oliver |
| Sophie | Rafferty |
| Sheila | Raymond |
| Tiffany | Sebastian |
| Yolanda | Stuart |
| Zola | Zane |

KEY GOALS:
*Wisdom. Experimentation. Service.*

## First Name Number 9

Your goal in life is to use your creative gifts to inspire and uplift humanity; you may be a wonderful musician, artist, actor or writer, or a passionate politician. You love helping others and physically demonstrating goodwill – giving is what makes the world go around and you're hoping people will follow suit. You possess very high standards, and you may pressurize yourself (and others) to get things right. However, sometimes people get irritated when you constantly try to correct their grammar, spelling or speech, but you're learning to be more accepting. You may find it difficult to live up to people's expectations and at times you pull yourself apart because you don't feel good enough. You're learning to give yourself a jolly pat on the back when you know you've done your best.

You're broad-minded and adaptable, and you like to think you can fit into any social situation, and you do generally blend in and disappear in a crowd. Sometimes you wish you weren't such a good chameleon because you realize you need to learn to find your own identity. You possess impeccable manners and a polished etiquette, but you can be deliberately rebellious just to oppose the stifling pressures of conformity. People may be shocked by your antics but you're worldly and wise and you take people's reactions in your stride. Indeed, you like to be the master of the universe and you may set your own rules and regulations, but you're learning to follow the consensus and do what's best.

You like to feel inspired by life, and are drawn to reading books by people who have made a valuable contribution to life; you may aspire to write your own autobiography one day. You love to broaden your horizons by throwing yourself into life full on.

## Middle Names Number 9

You can learn to become your own best friend by developing rock-steady faith in yourself and your abilities. Perhaps you've previously been through situations where you felt all hope was lost and now you're ready to pick yourself up, dust yourself off and start again. This name can help to support you in focusing on what you're good at and playing on all your positive attributes. You're also learning to drop the arrogance because nobody likes a show-off.

This name is teaching you to start experimenting with life – there's so much more to do and learn, and a lot more you can achieve. Indeed, you can support your growth by giving yourself approval to do what you need to do because you're your own keeper. You possess a silly sense of humour, but you aim to make jokes about subjects or people that are harmless and fun. Learning to laugh helps you to use your energies creatively, especially at times when your lid's about to burst from all the pressures in your life. Developing cultural interests can support you to free up misconceptions as it  liberates you with facts that expand your horizon.

## Family Name Number 9

Over the generations your family have been working on the right use of power. For example, your father was a politician, your grandmother was a respected elder, and you are a judge, which are all powerful roles within society. Your family karma is teaching you to honour and obey your soul rather than surrendering to your individual cravings for power and influence. You are all learning to be humble, because everyone is capable of contributing towards society, but your family's responsibility is to set a good example to others.

Some family members may be highly judgemental and critical of others' behaviour and don't approve of some members of your group. For example, your cousin is a prostitute and your brother practises a different religion to the one you were born into. However, your family karma is teaching you to be more inclusive and to accept and honour the differences, because humanity is one soul and one life.

For generations your family may have worked ceaselessly to protect others' human rights. You may all feel passionately about politics, the arts, sport or religion, and your family may be only too pleased to enter emotional or intellectual battlefields if you think it will make a difference. Sometimes you may feel like the underdog in the family and you want to be given an equal chance to live up to your potential. At times you may preach on at each other about your views, values and beliefs – you're a bunch of idealists. Your home regularly plays host to some lively debates and all and sundry are welcome to join in with the fun and contribute their knowledge.

Your family are generally very good at discriminating facts, and are able to see the global picture and the cosmic reasoning behind situations. People may come to you all for knowledge or advice. However, whilst you're big softies on the inside you do offer people tough love because you tell it as it is. You're learning to listen to each other's wisdom because you may all think you know it all.

## Expression Number 9

In the past (or past lives) you may have been a spy who kept all your knowledge hidden in your mind or used your Mensa intelligence to outwit 'the enemy'. For example, you were an environmentalist who spied upon scientists' computer data for your own use in your argument about climate change. You kept this secret information to yourself, when it could have been of huge benefit to humanity had you exposed your findings. Now you're learning to get together openly with like-minded people in order to help solve your own problems and to find bigger solutions for the world.

Under pressure your head may feel heavy and your judgements clouded, and you may feel bitter towards your situation. You may pressure others into performing a song and dance, and your behaviour can be shockingly out of order. You can be like a rebel without a cause and get angry just for the sake of letting off steam; you're learning to channel your energies positively and creatively. Learning to be kind to yourself and compassionate with others can help to smooth your journey during times of change and transformation.

Your soul gift is your wisdom; you have been through the mill time and time again and now you possess a truly liberated view on life. You've a profound ability to be able to open others' eyes wide, particularly as they listen to your meaningful tales when you're narrating a story. Your main cause in life is to serve others and you are only truly happy when you know that others' needs are being met. Indeed, you're drawn to vocational 'work' and want to follow your soul's calling, and you seek to inspire others to jump on board and do the same. You sometimes moan on about all that's wrong with the world or you may be a real martyr, but you're learning to humbly accept that you can only change yourself and help to make the world a better place.

## Pet Names and Pseudonyms Number 9

People may call you by a Pet Name or Pseudonym Number 9 because it can help you to transform your life. Perhaps you currently feel like you are shedding an old skin and growing a new one, and that this name can help you to evolve. You may be given this name because people think you're a bit judgemental and they want you to learn to relax. They may also value your opinions at times, and it can help you to stay true to your values and principles.

You may feel uncomfortable with this name if you want to remain entrenched in the past because it helps you to let go and to expand your consciousness. You're learning to see the global vision so that you can make all the right moves. You may like this name because it makes you feel more intelligent or that you're an upstanding citizen of the world.

You may call people a Pet Name or Pseudonym Number 9 because you see them as charismatic, colourful and larger than life, or because they can cheer you up with their very existence. You may feel people know something you don't and you want them to spill the goodies. You may be looking to expand your awareness and may be attracted to use this name because of their knowledge, background or education.

You may call a person by this name when you want them to congratulate you on your achievements, or you want a pat on the head and a nod of approval. If you think people are being a little too perfect or superior, projecting this name may help them to come back to earth with a bump. You may call someone by this name when you can see they are fully in command of the ship, and you may be only too happy to sail along with them.

Chapter 5

# Name Changing

Numerology is a useful guide that helps you to choose your baby's names with awareness. Names influence you for a lifetime and so it's essential to find the best possible names for your baby's growth. Numerology helps you to connect with your baby and to recognize its needs, and can gently help to guide your baby towards its destiny. Through birth names your child can explore soul potential, gifts, challenges and lessons in life in its own unique way. At birth your baby is like an open book waiting for its story to be written.

Names can fit you like a glove and you feel completely at home with their vibrations, and at these times you're flowering with your potential and offering your true self to the world. Other names may not feel so comfortable; for example, you may feel that you cannot relate to some of the Pet Names that people call you at all. So what happens if your baby grows up rejecting the wonderful names you've so lovingly chosen? Perhaps your child feels embarrassed by the connotation of its name, for example, Sushi, Trouper or Sunshine? However, you may think it's the physical meaning of a name or its psychological label that causes all the problems and unrest, but it's actually the sound of the name vibrations that disturbs or enhances harmony. Ideally, it's best for your child to learn to make friends with their names, but if this isn't feasible and your child really needs to find other names then Numerology is here to help.

Name changing is popular in the Far East where they are highly superstitious and tend to project black-and-white meanings onto life. However, this creative tool is used in every corner of the world because people are always seeking new ways to explore life and to improve themselves. Indeed, you may find that changing your names gives you the opportunity to turn over a new leaf; you find yourself on a new page that opens up a whole new chapter in your life. Changing your names can inspire you, breathe fresh air into stagnant situations, and can help you to attract new people and energies into your life.

# Why Change Your Name?

Your full birth names (First Name, Middle Names and Family Name), together with your Date Of Birth, dominate your existence, and the influence of these vibrations is felt throughout the whole of your life. Your birth names take precedence over any newly acquired names because they are your first point of call, and contain your original seed potential. So why bother changing your names at all, if it only creates extra lessons and more work for you? Acquiring new names is useful because it gives you a new set of tools to help you explore the gifts and potential contained within your original birth chart, and for you to experience further growth. However, even if you change your names it's easy to revert back to the original birth names. Whilst this may create more paperwork you may come to the conclusion that one set of names (karma) is quite enough!

There are so many reasons why you or your child may want to change names. You may be trying to wipe out the past, to disassociate with aspects of yourself that you don't like, or you may be trying to run away from yourself. You may want to change your name in order to be more successful. For example, it has been suggested that Prince Charles was asked to consider changing his name to George VII when he ascends to the throne to avoid historical associations with past monarchs called Charles. Whilst overall it's always best to make the most of the names you've been divinely given, if you feel taking on new names can serve a good purpose and help you on the road to self-discovery, then it's your choice.

You may want to change your surname to your partner's Family Name when you get married, and this new name combination offers new potential for life, love and learning. If you do not want to take on your partner's name at marriage, perhaps it's because you're not ready to fully commit to the union or because you may feel your first commitment lies with your birth family. It may be that you are incredibly independent. However, when you get married both sets of Family Names are speaking to your subconscious mind and giving you clues about what you need and what's best for you to choose.

You or your child may be drawn to changing the way your name is used by others, if it can help to project a truer aspect of yourself. For example, Prince William's girlfriend is called Kate and it has allegedly been suggested that she prefers to be called by her full name Catherine. The name Kate adds up to a 10/1, which highlights independence. Catherine adds up to 47/11/2, which highlights loyalty, friendship, security and endurance. The Number 11 highlights the quality of service, passion and inspiration. Catherine's Name Number 47/11/2 is exactly the same number as Prince William's Life Path Number 47/11/2. This can potentially help to enhance their compatibility and their ability to relate to each other

If you ask people to call you by your Middle Name instead of your First Name, you may be missing out on your full potential. You may go through life feeling as though there's something missing or that your lights are permanently stuck on amber. However, when you are ready to embrace life fully you may want to revert back to using your First Name. For example, British ex-Prime Minister Gordon Brown was born James Gordon Brown. Gordon adds up to 37/10/1, which highlights leadership and a pioneering spirit. James adds up to 12/3, which highlights the potential ability to follow through on matters and get things done. Whilst your Middle Name(s) can support you throughout life, you may find that using your First Name helps you to maximize your potential and use your gifts, so you can walk to your natural rhythm.

Later in life you or your child may decide to use your gifts in the public arena, and you may need to choose Stage Names to help you to get in character or carry out your role.

These names may give you permission to explore other aspects of yourself, or to be someone else for a while – an entertainer, an actor, an artist, a doctor or musician. For example, supermodel Agyness Deyn was born Laura Hollins. Her Personality Number is a 7, which highlights introspection, but her Life Path Number is 3 and her year of birth adds up to another 3, which highlights confidence, creativity and self-expression. Her Stage Name Agyness Deyn also adds up to a 3 and the Family Name Deyn on its own is yet another 3. These new names are helping her to utilize the bubbly, extrovert energy already in her chart to help her overcome any shyness, so she can shine with confidence and utilize her creative gifts. These new Stage Names have worked particularly well for Laura because they are the same number (3) as in her original birth chart, but they may have helped to give her a push in the right direction.

Finally your child may want to change names if the name vibration is the same as your own (or your partner's) perhaps because there is pressure to live up to your achievements. For example, perhaps you are a super mum or an amazing dad, a successful writer, footballer, or ballet dancer, or you have found fame and fortune by using your business acumen. Perhaps one of the reasons you may have given your child the same name vibration is because you want to see your unfulfilled dreams and ambitions realized, or because you want to pass on your gifts to future generations. However, if you and your child share the same name vibration you can be wonderful mirrors for each other. It can help you both to recognize your qualities and gifts, and enable you both to see yourselves clearly. This is called soul work and the birth names provide opportunities for your child to develop a deeper connection to life. However, if your child does go on and changes their name, it can still help them address issues relating to their personal desires. Ultimately your child is learning to be at one with him- or herself on a very personal journey.

# So How Can Numerology Help You Change Your Names?

Changing names is an instinctive process for most people and you can just feel what's right. However, by looking at other numbers in your overall Birth Chart you can work more consciously with the process. For example, your First Name Jack adds up to a 7. Your Personality Number is a 2 and your Life Path Number is a 5. You may find a new First Name Number that adds up to a 2 to help you explore issues relating to your personality characteristics, or choose a First Name Number 5 to help you explore the soul gifts and issues relating to your bigger purpose or path in life. Perhaps you may even choose a new First Name that adds up to the same number as Jack (7), but one that contains a different sequence of numbers and that adds different flavours to the same recipe.

### Missing Number Clues

You or your child can also change your name to a number that's missing from your overall birth names. For example, Lily Ann Trump has the numbers 6 and 8 missing from her full

Birth Names; she may decide to find new names that add up to one or both of these Missing Numbers.

### LILY ANN TRUMP
3937  1 5 5  2 9 3 4 7

Numbers that are missing contain hidden clues about gifts you possess but that you may have been hiding under a bushel. For example, you may think you're hopeless at cooking and dine out all the time. You constantly criticize your own attempts, which only enhances your incapability. By looking at your full birth names you may be surprised to discover a Missing Number 3, which highlights creative flair and inspiration. Recognizing and identifying your Missing Numbers can help you to reconnect with your gifts and help you to release outmoded mindsets. Self-awareness can help you to maximize your potential in all areas of your life.

# The Initials

Many people add an initial or letter to their names to alter the overall vibration. For example, Richard E Grant, George W Bush, P Diddy. The initial is like a name unto itself and the qualities it contains influence all the other names. For example, the Stage Name P Diddy. P is a 7, which highlights progressive thinking and the ability to make things happen. Diddy adds up to a 28/10/1, which highlights business flair and originality. So the number 7 enhances the 28/10/1 vibration; it may help Diddy to remain one step ahead of the game in business.

Adding an initial to your names can help you or your child to explore hidden qualities or help you to exteriorize your gifts. Like changing any name, adding an initial can make the world of difference to your experiences in life and so it's important you choose carefully.

## Generic Initials

You or your child may choose to add other generic initials or letters to your names to empower yourself in different situations. For example, 'Mr' adds up to a 13/4, which highlights seriousness and responsibility. 'Mrs' adds up to 14/5, which highlights knowledge and magnetism. 'Miss' adds up to 15/6, highlighting warmth and wisdom. 'Master' adds up to 22/4, which highlights determination and sensitivity. 'Ms' adds up to 5, highlighting common sense and clear communication. By adding these prefixes to your names it may alter your mood, the way you think and act, or help to enhance your spiritual growth, which is the same as with taking on any new name. It's good to be aware of the different name derivations that you use and the types of circumstances you encounter when using them because experience is the best teacher.

## Consulting the Professionals

*Choose the Perfect Baby Name* can give you an abundance of information to help you choose your baby's names. However, a professional Numerologist can help you with your quest to find the best possible names for your baby because they are able to see the bigger picture. A Numerologist can help you or your child to find new First, Middle and Family Names, and also new Initials, Stage Names, Business Names or Pseudonyms. Numerology can help you and your child to be at peace with yourselves, and by feeling at one with your names you may find more fulfilment in life.

# Missing Numbers 1 to 9

Missing numbers offer you clues about gifts or qualities that you have good working knowledge of from the past (or past lives). Work out your missing number(s) from your full birth names (see Chapter 3) to see if you recognize or feel that you or your baby identify with any of these key traits.

1  You're a natural leader, ambitious, forthright and determined, and you've learned to value yourself and your abilities. You're courageous. You possess a warrior-like ability to conquer problems and overcome your own limitations in life. You're a strategic planner who masterminds each and every next move.

2  You're a stabilizing force in others' lives because you've learned to measure situations carefully and to stay centred during emotional storms. You're a natural at mediating because you're able to see both sides and compromise. You're sensitive and can feel others' pain, but you allow others to make their own decisions.

**3** You're able to express yourself in many different ways. You're a natural observer of life. You've learned to take life as it comes, and this attitude helps you to make the most of situations. You possess creative flair and you often inspire others. You like to keep yourself busy. You are able to finish what you start.

**4** You've learned to take responsibility for yourself, and you know you're able to survive, no matter what. You like to build solid friendships and are always there for your workmates. You provide a rock-steady influence in others' lives during times of crisis. You've learned to be reliable and to work hard for what you want.

**5** You're able to communicate with everyone, and somehow you understand what is being said even when you don't speak the language. You're naturally perceptive but you give away little of what you know; you like to give people the facts. You're spontaneous and you've learned to embrace change.

**6** You've learned to put others' needs before your own. You're a natural provider and you take great pleasure in looking after your team. Your emotional honesty helps to draw people closer together. You're like a wise owl because you take a bird's-eye view of situations so that you can make the best choice.

**7** You are able to walk your talk; being true to yourself is what makes life worthwhile. You've learned to be grateful for your opportunities in life, and you like to show others appreciation. You're naturally intuitive, and you're able to use this gift to illuminate the truth.

**8** You've learned to stand up on your own; you're spiritually strong and provide for your own material needs. You re-evaluate life constantly, which helps to keep your life flowing. You are able to make a success out of nothing because you take responsibility and learn by your mistakes; you empower others to do the same.

**9** You have faith in life and you live in hope, which is a constant source of inspiration to others. You have learned to be adaptable and get along with everyone. You're wise and giving and you help people in any way you can. You're passionate about equality and you treat everyone the same.

# Letter Initials A–Z

Adding a letter or initial into your sequence of names makes an enormous difference to you and your baby's potential. You can identify key traits below but these qualities blend with the rest of your name so take a look at the whole picture, and use your intuition to help you choose. You can find clues about each Letter Initial in the alphabetical list below.

### A = 1

You may be drawn to using this initial because you want to project your leadership abilities, or because you want to be put on a pedestal. You may be looking for direction or want to be brought out of yourself. At present you may be stuck in old ways of thinking, but this vibration can help you develop a new attitude towards life.

### B = 2

You may be drawn to using this initial because you want to project your softer side or because you want to be treated with kindness. You may be looking for people to relate to emotionally. At present you may be indecisive, but this vibration can help you to weigh up situations carefully.

### C = 3

You may be drawn to using this initial because you want to project that you're footloose and fancy free, or because you want abundance. You may be looking for ways to relax. At present you may want to be the centre of attention. This vibration can help you to recognize what you're doing or help you to accept yourself.

## D = 4

You may be drawn to using this initial because you want to project that you're efficient and orderly, or because you want to be clear about your boundaries. You may be seeking energy and motivation in order to carry on. At present, your foundations may be shaky; this vibration can help you to address practical needs.

## E = 5

You may be drawn to using this initial because you want to project your popularity, or to promote your services. You may be looking to carry out some research. At present you may be unreliable. This vibration can help you to develop common sense so that your life can function and flow.

## F = 6

You may be drawn to using this initial because you want to project more love into the world, or because you want to feel loved and wanted. You may want to be a part of a group. At present you may feel let down by others. This vibration can help you to see beyond the surface.

## G = 7

You may be drawn to using this initial because you want to project integrity or because you want to learn to be able to trust. You may be looking for solitude or want some space. At present you may feel anxious; this vibration can help you to connect to the truth.

## H = 8

You may be drawn to using this initial because you want to project an elevated status, or because you want to develop inner strength or become more assertive. You may be looking for a father figure to take control of your life. At present you may be stubborn; this vibration can help you to surrender, stop struggling and do what's best.

## I = 9

You may be drawn to using this initial because you want to project intelligence and superiority, or because you want to be able to judge situations correctly. You may be looking for an identity. At present you may feel in limbo. This vibration can help you to make decisions based upon facts.

## J = 10/1

You may be drawn to using this initial because you want to project focus and determination, or because you want to achieve your goals. You may be looking for a breakthrough. At present you may be naïve. This vibration can help you to sit up and pay attention to reality.

## K = 11/2

You may be drawn to using this initial because you want to project passion and inspiration, or because you're seeking clarity. You may be looking for a message from above. At present you may feel a failure; this vibration can help encourage you to keep on using your gifts.

## L = 12/3

You may be drawn to using this initial because you want to project generosity, or because you're looking for ways to give. You may want to be able to move on with your life. At present you may find it hard to concentrate; this vibration can help you to focus on one thing at a time.

## M = 13/4

You may be drawn to using this initial because you want to project fundamental change, or because you want to take your awareness to a new level. You may be looking for opportunities to grow. At present you may be locked into dramas. This vibration can help you to express yourself and be practical.

## N = 14/5

You may be drawn to using this initial because you want to project specific information, or because you're seeking knowledge. You may be looking for clarity. At present you may feel restricted; this vibration can help you to discover why, and to find freedom within.

## O = 15/6

You may be drawn to using this initial because you want to project care and protection, or because you want to feel loved and nurtured. You may be looking for justice. At present you may feel resentful over your duties. This vibration can help you to make choices in life.

### P = 16/7

You may be drawn to using this initial because you want to project team spirit, or because you want to grab hold of every opportunity. You may be seeking time for reflection. At present you may feel used; this vibration can help you to say 'no' and to reflect on life, and make your choices.

### Q = 17/8

You may be drawn to using this initial because you want to project honesty, or because you're waking up to the truth. You may be looking for a spiritual path or direction. At present you may be introspective. This vibration can help you to materialize your dreams.

### R = 18/9

You may be drawn to using this initial because you want to project inclusiveness, or because you want to feel above the rest. You may want to experiment with life. At present you may be stifled by your own rules and regulations. This vibration can help you to let go of the past.

### S = 19/10/1

You may be drawn to using this initial because you want to project wisdom and vision, or because you want to get to the very top. You may be buzzing with new ideas. At present you may be highly self-critical; this vibration can help you to accept yourself fully.

### T = 20/2

You may be drawn to using this initial because you want to project a sense of cooperation, or because you want someone to hold your hand. You may be looking for a soul mate. At present you may be emotionally demanding. This vibration can help you to share.

### U = 21/3

You may be drawn to using this initial because you want to project joy, or because you want to be more enthusiastic about life. You may be looking for entertainment. At present you may be careless. This vibration can help you to monitor your actions so that you become more productive.

### V = 22/4

You may be drawn to using this initial because you want to project your practical achievements, or because you want to go back to the drawing board. You may be looking to join forces with others. At present you may feel indecisive; this vibration can help you to take practical steps forwards.

### W = 23/5

You may be drawn to using this initial because you want commitment, or because you want to change direction in life. You may want to be able to communicate. At present you may feel distracted. This vibration can help you to connect with your soul and gain clarity.

## X = 24/6

You may be drawn to using this initial because you want to project harmony, or because you want to find peace within yourself. You may be looking for love and security. At present you may feel time-pressured; this vibration is helping you to manage your life successfully.

## Y = 25/7

You may be drawn to using this initial because you want to project that you get results, or because you want to be more productive. You may want to communicate with people at a deep level. At present you may feel isolated; this vibration can help you to connect with people and life.

## Z = 26/8

You may be drawn to using this initial because you want to project compassion and strength, or because you may want to be respected. You may be competitive. At present you may be tempestuous; this vibration can help you to take prime responsibility for your life.

# Chapter 6

# Fine-Tuning the Name Numbers

**W**hen searching for names for your baby it's useful to find information that can help you make the best choice. The numbers 1 to 9 are more potent than the double-digit numbers (for example, 21, 47, 56) because they form the foundations of all life. They are potent because all the memories of the past, the present and the potential for the future are condensed within them.

However, the double digits bring to light the finer details regarding your baby's strengths, challenges and potential in life. So, for example, you may be thinking about naming your new baby girl Anna, which adds up to a 12/3. You can read about this name in Chapter 4, 'Names Decoded'. You can then go on and read more about Anna's name under the double-digit heading, '12/3' in this chapter. Anna is also listed in Chapter 8, '100 Popular Baby Names', so you can find information there too.

The single-digit numbers give you the general 'weather forecast' and the double digits can offer you a more local reading. When you bring them together it can help to refine the outlook of any baby's name; it's like looking through a wider lens where you are able to see more detail. As always, allow your intuition to help you read between the lines so that you can obtain an overall feel for the name in order to find the perfect name for your child.

You can look up any name in this chapter: First Name, Middle Name, Family Name, Stage Name or Pet Name, and Expression Name Numbers too.

# Name Number 1

### 10/1

You can be naïve beyond belief, but even though you've been through the mill in the past you do try to stay positive. You can be stubborn and selfish at times. You're good at recognizing your shortcomings and you possess enough wisdom to be able to change your behaviour. You're full of vitality and purpose, and you have a powerful intellect. You may fight to be right, but you're learning to stick with your opinions rather than being bulldozed down by what others want you to think, say or do. Some days you can be self-conscious and withdrawn, but you're learning to take advantage of these periods to help you gain useful insights into life.

### 19/10/1

You're worldly and wise, and you love narrating true-life stories because they bring out compassion in others and demonstrate the common thread of unity. You possess high standards and ideals and you pressurize yourself to achieve your goals; you aim far above and beyond what you have ever accomplished before. You're easily disappointed with life, particularly when others fail to make your grade, but you're learning to accept that everyone can only do their best. You're dynamic and strong-willed. Your magnificence shines through when you're focusing on worthwhile causes or making a valuable contribution to life. You sometimes act all innocent to avoid hurting others' feelings, but you find it impossible to tell lies. You're learning to stick to the facts.

## 28/10/1

You are bold, courageous and determined, and you're focused on creating success in all areas of your life. Your internal radar system is able to track down all the components you need to succeed. Many of your sentences start with, 'I want,' as you lay your claim to life and believe it is your right. You're learning to surrender to your higher will, and to follow a path that can provide you with soul growth and your material needs. You may be superb at organization or great at business, but you know there's always so much more to learn in life. You may be a natural entrepreneur, but at times you sabotage your plans by procrastinating. Failure means not trying, so you're learning to grow up, take responsibility, and go for life.

## 37/10/1

You're gentle, kind, and physically demonstrative, and you love spending time outdoors or in nature. You may also be dreamy and get lost in your imagination but you're learning to stay focused on reality. You're great at multi-tasking and you're multi-talented too, but you need to keep your mind positive and hold the vision in order to harness your gifts and manifest your dreams. In the past you may have opted out of life or vaguely followed others because you were directionless. Instead of sitting on the fence you're learning to trust life. You're brimming with self-confidence, and you love expressing your creative gifts. Your clear-cut sense of humour brings tears of joy to people's eyes – you're a natural entertainer.

## 46/10/1

You're a hands-on helper and you do your best to bring love and warmth into people's lives, and you may often give up your leisure time to support others. You possess an inventive mind and you set about grounding your ideas so that they can be of practical use to the world. Your goal in life is to provide a comfortable lifestyle for yourself and your loved ones, and you work hard to maintain your efforts and ensure needs are met. You may be materialistic or focus too much attention on what's on the surface. You're learning to value love and respect. You're strong-willed, but duty-bound and team-spirited so you generally choose to do what's best.

## 55/10/1

You enjoy flirting and getting a 'free' taster of life, but you may find making or keeping commitments challenging. Whilst you're open to life's opportunities you eventually need to choose a direction. You're clear at giving instructions, but you can be pushy and aggressive sometimes. You're learning to value constructive feedback and to alter your behaviour or attitude if need be. You may be an adrenalin junkie but life in the fast lane may wear you out. You're learning to withdraw into your mind to find more constructive solutions to your restlessness, boredom, and to the emptiness inside. You're soulful, sensitive and perceptive and you instantly pick up on others' thoughts. You're happy to pass on your knowledge and observations to help stimulate others' growth in life.

### 64/10/1

You're group-orientated and you may find it impossible to consider your own needs without including others. You enjoy spreading your time and wealth around because you love giving. The need for material security may motivate you and drive you forwards, but you're learning to value all the learning experiences you have in life. You are easily satisfied and contented when in the company of good friends and family and you may lack impetus at these times. You're learning to make an effort. You may feel life is your oyster but you absolutely know it's an open book waiting to be discovered and explored. Some days you may allow your pioneering spirit to get the better of you as you disappear off into the distance; your actions may alter others' direction in life too.

### 73/10/1

You feel a strong pull towards your spirituality, but you're constantly analysing everyday situations to discover what life's about on the material plane too. You possess visionary skills and you're a forward planner who always likes to be one step ahead of the game. You're learning how to relax. You're fun-loving and playful but sometimes you throw a spanner in the works by messing things up, but you're learning to concentrate. You prefer to focus on materializing your goals and making things happen rather than indulging in idle chat. You practise positive thinking or creative visualization to keep your mind on track. You're prolifically creative and a busy bee so you really value meditation or quiet times when you can recharge your batteries.

## 82/10/1

You may feel as though the whole of life is new to you, or you may feel different in your skin to others. Perhaps you experience vivid flashbacks from the past (or past lives). You may not recognize yourself as you are now but you can recognize the important lessons you are learning. You're learning to live life for today, and also to participate in the process without needing to direct or control every move. You may be a powerful teacher and often reflect enlightenment to others, often without knowing it. You know how to stand up for yourself but you may prefer to opt for passivity as your main line of defence. You struggle with your intellect, but as long as you're learning and growing all is well.

## 91/10/1

You allow yourself to be led through life by your inner wisdom, but you may also be stubborn and refuse to listen to others' guidance at times. You're a natural leader because you believe in yourself and your abilities. Sometimes you set rules and regulations that others find difficult to follow, but you can be extremely reasonable, compassionate and kind. You're a high achiever but you feel hopeless when you're unable to perform simple tasks, like baking a cake. However, you enjoy the process of gathering fodder from all your experiences and integrating them within your mind. You tend to point your finger at people, but you're keen on self-improvement and are happy to 'pull your socks up' when necessary too.

# Name Number 2

### 11/2

You're passionate about life and give yourself over completely to all that you do, whether it's playing baseball for your country, cleaning your car, or looking after your child. You desire to do things well, but you're disappointed with life when it doesn't live up to your standards of perfection. You feel your emotions intensely but you're learning to carry on doing and giving of your best, and this in itself can help to keep you calm. Utilizing your creative gifts and finding simple ways that you can make a contribution to life is a motivating force; it gives you a good reason to get out of bed each day. Your goal is to see your own life as part of a much bigger picture and to connect with your spirituality, so that you feel more at one with life.

### 20/2

You're a sensitive soul but you try to surround yourself with 'tough skin' that protects you from getting hurt. You're learning to work through your fears, so that you can throw caution to the wind and open yourself up to life. When you feel secure and centred, your inner wisdom rises to the surface to be used so your soul can sing. You're attentive to others' needs. You're able to feel what's going on in your environment and to relate to people emotionally. You're a good negotiator, but you're learning that successful negotiations often require compromise. You're also learning to let go of emotional attachment to fulfilling your desires so that you can feel at peace.

### 29/11/2

You fear failure on any level so your goal is to reach the highest levels of achievement. You may be an icon in sport, the arts or entertainment, or receive recognition for your gifts. You may be over-sensitive and temperamental, but you're learning to be more decisive and to keep on trying. You're also learning to let go of self-preoccupation and focus your energy on collective goals and needs. You possess strong values and beliefs but you're broadminded and welcome others' opinions. You enjoy debating important issues because it expands your awareness and helps you to learn more about life. You're warm and loving, and you may seek out a soul mate so that you can share your life with that special one.

### 38/11/2

You're warm, charming and engaging, and people are magnet-ically drawn to you because you're so self-assured and help them feel at ease. You're highly ambitious and you push yourself with a force in order to succeed in life. You can be indecisive or easily distracted by all the copious amounts of daily activities. You're learning to re-evaluate life regularly and to be assertive so that you can stay on top of the game. You're abundantly expressive and creative and you're a natural entertainer, but you're learning to laugh at yourself too because you can be serious. You're edgy and live off your nerves. Your goal is to connect with spirituality; it gives you the inner strength to address issues and transform your life.

## 47/11/2

Your goal in life is to manifest your dreams and also to enjoy helping others to make their dreams come true. You are realistic about what it's possible to achieve but you do allow yourself to daydream, which actually helps you to clarify your vision. You possess staying power and physical endurance, and you beaver away endlessly at life. You're nature-loving, gentle and kind, and you love observing all the different cycles in nature and in your own life. You may be drawn to philosophy, psychology and spirituality or possess altruistic interests; you're a deep thinker. At times you may rush into situations, but you're learning to weigh up your options carefully before making decisions and arriving at the final destination.

## 56/11/2

You're a people person and a team player, and may enjoy the role of manager. You're highly intellectual, but your mind takes you to deeper levels of spiritual awareness and the clarity you gain illuminates all areas of life. Your goal is to be able to share your wisdom and knowledge with others. You possess sharp communication skills and succinctly deliver messages that can touch people's hearts. You're learning to compromise and enjoy negotiating. You're acutely sensitive so at times you protect yourself by keeping your distance emotionally. You're attractive and popular; by letting go of control and falling hopelessly in love, you can see the light. You're great at networking and you're always spinning around inspiring others with your creativity.

## 65/11/2

You like to please people and keep them happy, and you may relish responsibilities. You're learning to nurture and care for your own needs because you tend to forget yourself at times. You love to regularly join forces with a group of friends or with teammates, where you can cook up ideas about projects you can all work on together. Whilst you may possess great managerial skills and know exactly how to make the best of people's talents, you're learning to listen to intuition. You're inquisitive and you want to be able to make sense of life at a deeper level. Your goal is to use your communication skills to benefit others.

## 74/11/2

Your goal in life is to keep instigating change. This may be particularly so when your routine or attitude has become jaded or when you find yourself dragged down by material concerns. You may sometimes hide behind the truth, but you're learning to take a step at a time and to trust that it all works out accordingly. You possess a refined taste in music, art, food and literature, and you may apply your sensitivity by working with colour. You may crave peace, and you aim to live a simple lifestyle where everything's above board and plain to see. You're loving, loyal and reciprocative, but you're learning to trust yourself because you can sometimes be naïve. You're a good listener and wonderful at uplifting others' spirits.

## 83/11/2

You may be a successful social entrepreneur but you hardly notice your achievements because you're too busy progressing goals. Your main goal is growth; you may take up personal and professional development in order to acquire practical skills that can support you in life. You may enjoy writing, painting, cooking or architecture, and through your work you may be able to communicate with the masses. You take responsibilities seriously; you've grown up and realize that everything comes with a price. You're learning to have fun creatively, and to enjoy playful expression in many different ways for no reason other than pure relaxation. You may be able to see beyond the present, and therefore people often seek you out for guidance.

## 92/11/2

You're constantly updating your skills; you love education and your goal is to make sure that people receive all the information they need. You possess impossibly high standards and you can be a hard task-master at times, but you're learning to accept life's little imperfections. You may be interested in the environment, humanitarian issues, and in subjects that are common to humanity. You're service-orientated and may inspire others. You may often feel that your life's in limbo. You're learning to call upon inner strength during periods of transformation so that you can find all the answers that you need. You're learning to relate to people emotionally and to feel comfortable in your own skin.

# Name Number 3

## 12/3

You're childlike and playful, with a wicked sense of humour. You're a natural exhibitionist but sometimes you go to great lengths to ensure you're centre stage. Perhaps you may wear flirtatiously daring outfits or deliberately say things to get attention; you're learning to weigh up situations and recognize what you're doing. You're warm and demonstrative, and you love connecting with friends over coffee and joining social groups because you need interaction. You may sometimes find it difficult to express deep emotion or to say, 'I love you.' The way you show you care is by practically doing things for others, like giving birth(!), cooking meals, writing reports, tidying the house or garden, and so on. Your goal is to learn to use your creative talents constructively.

## 21/3

You're wise but you're always seeking ways to learn more about life. In the past you may have been cynical or resentful about things you didn't have and wanted, but you're learning to give over and follow your divine purpose in life. You're placid, kind and receptive, and a natural counsellor who really listens to what people say. You're ambitious and focused on achieving your goals. If you've experienced luck and prosperity in your life it's probably because you've worked for it! You're learning to count your blessings. You may be fiercely independent, or detached and aloof, but you're learning to get involved and to keep on giving.

## 30/3

You're always ready for action, and like a backpacker who travels the world you're prepared to go with the flow. Whilst 'All roads lead to Rome', following 'sheep' can sometimes lead you astray. You're learning to reflect upon your actions, so that you can ascertain which road you need to take, and go on towards your destination. Your goal is to learn to master the art of multi-tasking because you're a busy bee and it can help you to be more productive. You're also learning how to find stillness and make time for rest and relaxation each day. You may be very sporty and enjoy outdoor activities because you feel free, and because you enjoy the social contact. You're prolifically creative, and you may always be making things with your hands. You're learning to express yourself fully.

## 39/12/3

You may be the recipient of inherited wealth. You're learning to be positive, to be more giving, and to acknowledge the abundance in life. You laugh a lot but you don't suffer fools gladly; you're wise beyond your years and you've really lived. You're generally tolerant, but you're learning to accept people even when they keep different standards or hold a different set of morals. When you notice something's out of place you swiftly take action, but you're also learning to recognize when it's best to leave things be. You're good at critical evaluation, and you're able to tap into your intellectual textbook of knowledge in order to help guide others. You take life in your stride and make the most of each day. Perhaps you sometimes feel that life's like one big holiday.

### 48/12/3

You like to keep active and you enjoy going to the gym, working hard and also seriously socializing. You like to progress situations until they reach their full potential. So if you're learning a new skill you may sit exam after exam until there are no more qualifications left on the subject, and then you move on. You may be psychic or be aware of the spiritual dimension to life. Perhaps you also believe in fate. You're generally astute and you read all the small print in contracts and refuse to be rushed through negotiations or into agreements. Your goal is to complete one situation before you move onto the next. You're learning to take life in your stride and to carry on regardless.

### 57/12/3

You love travelling because it allows you to meet new people, to learn new skills, and to discover new and exciting informa-tion that you can pass on to others. You love all the details in life. You're like a private detective systematically delving deeper into situations until you reach the jackpot – you want to find out the truth. You're learning to make contact with your soul, which is your most reliable informant. You're great at throwing people off-scent or covering up your actions, but at times your carefree attitude gives you away. You're realizing that there are no real secrets any more because the world has seen and done it all before, and just like everyone you also have important lessons to learn. Your goal is to keep your mind occupied and to keep busy – then you're happy.

### 66/12/3

Your soul is uplifted when you spend quality time with friends and family, and when you listen to beautiful music or visit an art gallery. Your life may lovingly revolve around providing care and comfort for others, which you enjoy even though you find it exhausting sometimes. You're learning to manage your time-keeping well so that you can create more harmony in your life. You're driven to create perfection in everything you do. Perhaps you're fussy about what you eat, or obsessive about the way you look and the appearance of your home. Your goal is to learn to value inner beauty rather than the superficialities of life. You may be incredibly sentimental, and so find it difficult to let go of the past. You're learning to find joy in the present.

### 75/12/3

You're a deep thinker and you enjoy pushing yourself beyond your intellectual limitations so that you can discover new facts about life. You're witty and perceptive, and you're able to use vocabulary concisely and effectively to get messages ashore. Your goal is freedom of expression, and you may travel with the wind if it means you can be yourself as your soul and also as nature intended. You enjoy swimming, meditating and partying, but you love playing sudoku, trivia games and joining in quiz nights at the pub. You're constantly using your creativity, and enjoy finding ways to help you lead a healthier and happier lifestyle. You can be over-sensitive and emotional at times, but your strong logic helps you to reason with yourself so that you can see the light.

## 84/12/3

You like the idea of being able to wander wherever life takes you, but you also like to know where you're going to sleep at night so you may be drawn to roaming closer to home. You may see the whole world like neighbours where everyone is free to pop into other countries for a cup of tea. You feel fortunate because you know you can look after yourself and you can survive life's ups and down. Perhaps you've made your pot of gold and lost it many times over. You're learning to take a more easy come, easy go attitude to life, in order to help you release heavy burdens and enjoy yourself. You may possess business flair and are particularly drawn to the creative arts. Your goal is to be successful.

## 93/12/3

You're socially and politically motivated. You think you can see all the reasons behind how and why events occur, and you want to correct them. You may want to change the world but you're learning to start with yourself by recognizing all the ways in which you can become a better person. You're compassionate and kind and you inspire others with your ability to give selflessly. You enjoy experimentation. You've no hang-ups about your body because you see it as a practical instrument that enables you to experience life and change. You're extremely capable, but your goal is to learn to ask for help because everyone has needs.

# Name Number 4

### 13/4

Your aim is to materialize your creative goals and to express yourself abundantly. You possess a knack of being able to conjure up original ideas, but you may feel confused about which ideas will work in reality, or dither about following them through. You're practical and hardworking, and you are more than capable of working on many different projects at once. You're learning to take a day at a time so that you can become more productive and safely progress on to your next phase in life. You possess an ambitious streak that sometimes urges you to leap in and take risks. You're generally steady and predictable but friends may be shocked by some of your antics. You believe in the maxim, 'no pain, no gain', and you're happy with the reward – spiritual growth, material resources, and freedom.

### 22/4

You're very thoughtful and kind and you want to please others. You may also be fragile emotionally and protect yourself from being hurt by being defensive and shutting people out of your life. You're learning to open up and share yourself, so that your soul wisdom can shine through and people can get close to the real you. You may be naturally cautious and weigh up endlessly before making decisions. You're also practical and once you see the bigger picture you do get on with the job efficiently. Your goal is to find your inner sense of security. You may get locked into situations, friendships or a monotonous routine because you resist change. You're learning to master your fears and adapt to life by laying down new structures that can support your growth.

### 31/4

You've a powerful mind and you're great at solving problems. Your goal is to practically improve life for yourself and others. You're very comfortable speaking up for people's rights or campaigning for your community; you aim to make a difference. At times you may be troubled by inner conflicts, which leave you feeling dazed and confused, or result in you being disorganized. You possess a fighting spirit. Like a long-distance runner you attain your goals by finding pure mental focus and physical endurance to crack on with reality. You're fun-loving, sociable and easy-going but you're extremely serious and responsible when it comes to the big issues in life. You enjoy physical contact and you're learning to be a loyal friend.

### 40/4

You're responsible, orderly and conscientious and adopting this manner helps you to consistently achieve your goals. You may be preoccupied with basics – diet, exercise, money, property, home and routine – but you're steadily building your empire. You work hard to maintain solid foundations in your life. You dislike surprises because they threaten your structure and force you back into survival mode, and you may be over-dramatic at times. You're able to break out of the heavy cage you sometimes build around yourself and are learning to embrace change. You like to feel special, but you're learning to find enjoyment in ordinary everyday things. Your goal is to utilize your passion and creativity in order to uplift yourself and enjoy life.

### 49/13/4

You're idealistic about life, which at least gives you a standard to aim for and ensures that you always give of your best. Sometimes you do give yourself a 'headache' by criticizing yourself and your achievements – even when you've performed well. It's your prerogative to change your point of view once you've assimilated new facts.

You're learning to bring more joy into your life. You're also learning to dissolve outmoded patterns of behaviour by recognizing what you do and altering your course if necessary. You're waking up and taking responsibility for your life because you know it's you who needs to put in effort if you want to achieve results. You're learning to be adaptable to change so that your whole life can run more smoothly.

### 58/13/4

You may enjoy living off your adrenaline and experiencing life on the edge, but you're down to earth and you know that the highs can't last forever. You're always re-evaluating in order to find ways of bringing more excitement and adventure into everyday life. Your goal is stability but you're on a fast track to spiritual growth, and you forge ahead with life because you know there's a lot of work to be done. You're perceptive and agile, and you mainly manage to move around life unscathed because you can think your way out of situations. You may also lead people a merry dance at times because you're a smart cookie. You can learn to change your fate by being upfront and assertive.

### 67/13/4

You're charitable, generous and giving, and you love contributing time and energy to community projects. You're devoted to your family and friends, and you stand right by their side through thick and thin. You're also learning to give people space because sometimes you may interfere and take on their problems. You're brutally honest, and whilst people respect you telling the truth you're learning to become more aware of people's feelings. You may avoid facing reality. Your goal is to keep on with life even if you feel you're weighed down with emotions, because eventually you find a way back up. You may want to heal the world but you're learning to love life's little imperfections, and to carry on healing yourself.

### 76/13/4

You believe in fairness and justice, and you're an anchor for others because you're honest and your feet are on the ground. You're team-orientated. Perhaps, for example, you take it on board to sort out all your family's legal affairs because you are able to see the bigger picture. You can sometimes be emotionally demanding and draining, but you're learning to respect others' needs and to be happy to offer them breathing space. You love to stage-manage events and you know how to present opportunities in a positive light. You're a fast mover but your goal is to be patient with yourself and trust life. You place strong parameters around yourself for protection, but you're learning to relax and enjoy life.

### 85/13/4

You generally take a black-and-white attitude towards life, but you can learn a lot by communicating with people and it can positively change your perspective. You tend to fight your battles with words. You're so sharp-witted and observant and good at clarifying situations, and you know how to avoid conflicts. You may experience a spiritual wake-up call during your lifetime, or work through powerful situations that define your character. You possess a strong sense of purpose. You're magnetic and popular but you may get possessive with friends but you're learning to let go of control and give up ownership. Your goal is to learn to take responsibility for yourself. You're able to empower others to be strong for themselves instead of them relying upon you.

### 94/13/4

You possess enough knowledge and inner wisdom to 'build your own house from scratch', but you still need to renew your qualifications and improve efforts. People may think that you know it all, but they may be judging you by your achievements, and you're quick to point out their gifts too. You love monitoring people's speech or movements. You're good at teaching people important skills that they can use to improve their quality of life. At times you can be lazy and you allow others to do all your donkey-work but you're learning to dissolve old habits of a lifetime. Your goal is to make constructive use of your knowledge, which you aim to do because you're passionate about change.

# Name Number 5

## 14/5

You like to make your presence felt; you may make loud sounds as you move around a room, or dance and sing so that others can physically hear you. You have a bright twinkle in your eyes and you command people's attention and even when you simply walk into the room people notice you. You draw people to you like magnets and you're popular too. You're learning to be reliable and to remember to turn up to your many appointments. You enjoy being physically affectionate with loved ones, but you can be aloof and detached at times in order to keep others away. Your goal is to learn to think before you speak and act because you tend to get caught up in the minute and rush into situations. You're extremely sensual and are very aware of your sexuality. You're also perceptive and inquisitive. You're learning to be astute with material matters.

## 23/5

You possess an ultra-violet imagination – you're able to see through the thin veil of your eyes into other levels of reality. You may be telepathic or psychic, but your goal is to explore the unseen world – you love to communicate with your soul. You enjoy writing, art, music, massage and travelling, and you're learning to express your creativity fully. Sometimes people find it difficult to keep up with you because you're constantly changing your plans and the topic of conversation. Your mind is quick to wander but you're learning to concentrate. You're gregarious and fun-loving, and you want to experience as much in life as you can. You want to build a love nest for your own emotional security. You're learning to bond with others.

## 32/5

Your goal is to look for the positive in people and in life. Whilst you're generally an optimistic and sunny person, your easy-going nature means that sometimes you let people get away with the moon. You're learning to develop a strong sense of self-esteem and self-belief so you can remove yourself from destructive situations or change your behaviour if need be. You're highly sensitized and your emotions are as flimsy as butterfly wings; learning to rationalize and deal with concrete facts can help you to be more productive. You're a kind, loving and generous soul, which is why you're so popular, and are often the life and soul of the party.

## 41/5

You're ambitious, self-motivated and direct, but you achieve your goals through pure perseverance and determination. Your goal is to work hard to provide material security for yourself. You may at times become a workaholic but you're learning to free up time for other commitments. Whilst a jet-set lifestyle may excite and attract you, you generally operate best from a solidly structured routine. You're learning to feel comfortable within yourself and to get organized. You may speak many languages or utilize your people skills to help you get on in life. You're incredibly perceptive and you tend to tell it like it is. You may be blessed with an abundance of friends and money, which brings you the freedom you desire. Your life may be full of surprises, which keeps you on your toes.

## 50/5

You change direction as often as the wind, but you like to live your life on the pulse because it makes you feel so vital. You're restless, and are always screaming out for more stimulation because you need to feel the adrenalin pumping in your body. You're edgy and people may find that exciting, but you're learning to connect with your soul in order to find any real satisfaction in your life. By regularly tapping into your inner point of stillness you may feel more settled within yourself. It can also help you to hold onto a job, relationship, or to stick around in one place for longer than your normal time slot. You're interested in knowledge and education, and you may be brilliant at research and communication. Your goal is to explore life fully.

## 59/14/5

You may possess a distinctive voice that people find attractive. Perhaps you're able to put important messages across because of your powerful manner of speech. You possess a huge vocabulary yet you are able to communicate concisely. You're learning to become more aware of the energy behind your words in order to magnify your intentions and become more focused and productive. You may be an information junkie and you enjoy passing your knowledge on through teaching, writing books or songs, or by public speaking. Your goal is to free up any restrictive mind-sets so that you can experience life more fully. You're highly charged sexually, and you're learning to channel your creativity into projects that are worthwhile.

## 68/14/5

You like to paint words with pictures in your mind because it helps you get a grip on reality. You're a very visual person and you may be fascinated by photography, (interior) design and architecture. You're learning to dig deeper than the surface. You may expand your knowledge by studying the works of great writers or artists and want to get into their mind. You make it your mission to learn about different cultures, and you may spend a lifetime tracing your own family tree. You may be a successful entrepreneur. Your main concern is to build a team of happy workers and make sure they take home their fair share of the profits. You may be a philanthropist, or devote your time to charities or events that provide care for the community.

## 77/14/5

You are a complex character because you're intellectual and possess a scientific brain that leads you to question everything. You're also deeply connected to your spirituality. You goal is to be able to bring together the best of both worlds so that you can feel at ease with reality. Sometimes you communicate astounding truths (out of the blue) and it makes people react, but you're learning to trust your intuition and to use your speech wisely. You're multi-talented, and you're a master at making things happen and achieving your goals because you put in so much effort. You're bored easily and you may dive from one interest to the next looking for your next high. You're learning to stay true to yourself.

## 86/14/5

Your goal is to build an empire filled with people you know and love; in your eyes this may include the whole world. You're incredibly charismatic, warm and well-meaning, and you're a loyal friend. You're good at communicating, and you can be extremely persuasive when selling your services, including all your terms and conditions. Sometimes you resort to manipulative behaviour to get exactly what you want. You're learning to do what's best in situations so as to create more harmony in your life. You may experience powerful relationships or situations that shake your tree because you're learning big lessons in life. You're growing up; tough decisions become easier when you know they're right, but you're learning to listen to reason. Your soul knows what's best.

### 95/14/5

You aim to remain faithful to yourself and to those to whom you've made commitments. You're learning to live by your values. Whilst you naturally demonstrate your wisdom by setting a good example and getting on with life, you are sharply outspoken with issues that touch your soul. You sometimes put yourself on the line, and also put people on the spot when presenting them with the facts. Your goal is to experiment with life because there's so much to learn and so much richness and knowledge that you can pass on to others. You may feel that your life is constantly pushing you forwards and you're in a race. You're learning to relax and enjoy the beauty of spiritual transformation.

# Name Number 6

### 15/6

Your goal is to master the art of relationships, which gives you plenty to do in a lifetime! You surround yourself with people day and night because you find it so supportive. You love merging in with the group and welcome the fact that you're all in it together, helping each other, and pulling your weight. You may be emotionally needy, and resentful when people don't give you what you want, but you're learning to provide emotional security for yourself. You're analytical and perceptive, and you note every little detail about a situation, but you're learning to be able to take a step back so you can take a bird's-eye view. You can be extremely nice or naughty, but your soul is helping you to make sense of it all so that you can become truly wise.

## 24/6

You're a home-loving person, and all your practical efforts are directed towards providing a comfortable environment where you (and others) can thrive. You may at times prefer to focus on the material side of life because you find emotions difficult to handle. You may sulk, brood or stamp your feet, but people learn when it's best to leave you be. You're learning to examine your emotions, so that you feel safe and can open up to loved ones. Your goal is to achieve all your desires before you die, but you're learning that it's your soul steering the course, so see what happens. You like your skills to be put to good use, so the more duties you're offered the better you feel about yourself and your life. You're happy to make a contribution.

## 33/6

You're bubbly, outgoing and generous, and you're a big softie who wears your heart on your sleeve. You may find it easy to say, 'I love you,' or to hold hands, cuddle, and kiss your friends because you're so warm and loving. You get along with most folk and take life in your stride, but you can become too complacent at times. You accept people on face value but you're learning to be more reflective and to take actions when necessary. Your goal is to serve your family and community, and you may sacrifice your own needs to get a job done well. You're prolifically creative, and you may be interested in the arts, music, design, beauty and healthcare.

## 42/6

You aim to follow the golden rules in life because you want to be seen as a good human being. You may feel more comfortable leading a conventional lifestyle. You possess a strong work ethic and like to provide others with value for money. You love to please, and your goal is to help people in any way you can: counselling, DIY, book-keeping – you do the lot. Whilst you're normally the most reliable person in the team, you're learning to set your boundaries so that you can carry out all your necessary tasks successfully. You like to take one step at a time, and to develop stable friendships that provide comfort and nourishment throughout your life.

## 51/6

You're ambitious and focused on achieving your goals, but you're also willing to push yourself hard to provide a better life for your friends and family. You're a wise warrior who champions fairness and justice for the whole community. You may find it easy to communicate your needs, but your dry sense of humour and colourful vocabulary sometimes deliver mixed messages. You're learning to be more precise and direct. You're rational and sensible when choosing your friends. In terms of sex and sensuality you can easily be lured in and led astray until you remember to call on your governing intellect. You're learning to heal old heartbreaks by falling in love again. You can access deeper levels of love within yourself and express more love in all areas of your life.

## 60/6

You're a perfectionist and you work hard to deliver your very best. You sometimes get caught up in situations or taken over by events but you're learning to see the bigger picture. You possess strong self-preservation instincts and you may demand that people run around you day and night. You're learning to be more considerate towards others. You're romantic and eloquent in your speech, and perhaps you adore reading or writing poetry. You see the beauty in life but you're compassionate about members of society who need care and protection. You're a team supporter, and you're happy to take on board as many commitments as you can to embrace life. You're a real sweetie.

## 69/15/6

Your goal is to channel all your passion and creativity into projects you believe in, and you generally do give your heart and soul over to life. You can be selfless in the way you provide love and support for others. You use all the wisdom you possess to help you do what's right. Sometimes you can be obsessive about annoying little details that frustrate your achievements, but you're learning to accept when you've done your best and move on. You're a great friend because you're genuinely interested in what people have to say; you aim to treat everyone the same. You feel others' emotions. You're learning to use your sensitivity to help you communicate love and wisdom to the world.

## 78/15/6

Your goal is to keep yourself motivated so that you tackle important issues and situations head on. You may prefer to stay tucked up inside your comfort zone wishing the world would go away, but you're learning to grow up fast and face reality. You may be emotionally attached to money or materialism and you may love to parade your success and achievements. You're learning to break down the walls of illusion by connecting with your spirituality; you can see the truth and recognize yourself clearly. You're learning to bring that all-encompassing power of love into your life so that it can touch your heart, and you can blossom.

## 87/15/6

You're a fast learner and you're brilliant at processing information because you're prepared to introspect. Your mind is constantly re-evaluating situations. You're incredibly resourceful and you're able to dig down deep to find new and inventive solutions to problems. You're learning to put your knowledge to concrete use by constructively helping others when you can. Your goal is to bring more love and spirituality into everyday life. You may encourage people to work together as a team. You're extremely grateful for all your gifts and you may see life as a blessing; you're also learning to appreciate people's kindness. You may enjoy organizing community events and you go to extremes to ensure they're a big hit with everyone and a success for the cause.

## 96/15/6

Your goal is to view life from a completely different perspective to the one you originally possessed. You are learning to accept yourself in order to help you to turn your life around. You can be full of yourself at times or feel you're standing stories above the rest of humanity, but you're learning to recognize the greatness within everyone and to show humility. You really want to be loved and approved of by others. Whilst this makes you eager to please you're learning to respect your own opinions and honour yourself. You exude warmth and worldliness, and you're inclined to stick up for the underdog because you can see what they need. You're a real trouper.

# Name Number 7

## 16/7

You're warm, loving and friendly, and a great deal of your time is centred around your family and home. You adore animals and insist that all your pets are treated like part of the family, which they are. Children are naturally drawn to you because of your wonderful imagination, which enables you to connect with them at their level. You can be incredibly naïve, but you're learning to be more self-conscious so that you can see the role you're playing in creating your reality. Your goal is to create space for quiet time so you can centre yourself and become more productive. You're an opportunist and you like to get the most out of life, but you also want others to benefit from your achievements.

## 25/7

You're a thoughtful, kind and considerate soul, but you are learning to compromise in order to be more productive. You always see the best in people, but you feel quietly let down at times when people are being plain rude, but it helps you to explore reality. You're incredibly sensitive and fragile and your vulnerability means that you sometimes reveal too much of yourself to others, and they pick up on your frailties. You're learning to rationalize situations and also to connect with your intuition so that you can trust yourself about what you need. Your goal is to learn to hold your head up high, to walk your talk, and be true to yourself – no matter what.

## 34/7

You're happy-go-lucky and relatively carefree about the direction you take in life as long as you're growing spiritually. Perhaps one moment you're out socializing, and in the next you've got your head down concentrating on work, or completing mundane tasks. Your goal is to learn to be adaptable to life's ever-changing circumstances. You're responsible and socially conscious, and you only want and take what you need. You're good at making things with your hands, and you express yourself through an abundance of creativity. Your 'works of art' inspire people and they can feel your joy through what you do. You're a loyal friend and you dislike gossip. You're able to see through people and recognize the truth.

## 43/7

You're an active person who methodically organizes each day in advance so that you can be the most productive. Your ability to get things done yesterday is second to none. You tend to panic when life throws you off course but instead of running ahead and making mistakes, you're learning to stay calm and take one step at a time. You're incredibly restless and impatient. Your goal is to learn to withdraw and introspect so that you can steady yourself emotionally. Your spirituality can help you to find the strength to hold it all together. You're tenacious and you're not easily drawn to change your beliefs or alter course – your life is your business.

## 52/7

You're a lucid dreamer and your intuitive visions may inspire you to turn inwards towards your spirituality, where you gain much clarity about yourself and life. You're a powerful communicator and you want to share your knowledge with others. You spend time networking, teaching, or writing lectures or books (technical data on life instruction). You're great at research because your natural perceptiveness enables you to capture every detail, but you can be fussy and clinical about getting it just so. You're learning to use your inner wisdom to help you weigh up situations and keep life simple. Your goal is to be at peace with yourself, so honesty is your motivating force in life.

## 61/7

You're forever analysing situations, or sentimentally romanticizing about the past. You ask yourself, 'Remember the sweet smell of roses in granny's garden?' or, 'Remember my first kiss?' You latch onto feelings that comfort you in order to feel secure emotionally. Like an archaeologist who digs deep to find buried treasure, you like to discover the truth; it can be a valuable healing process too. You're always looking for signs from your environment to give you direction in life or to affirm you're on track. You're learning to do your best each day and to let life unfold naturally. Your goal is to learn to 'lose yourself' within a group and to make dreams come true.

## 70/7

You're a progressive thinker and a fast mover when it comes to materializing your goals. You're learning to keep your emotions in check in order to maximize your efforts; meditation, tai chi, or a gentle walk around the block can all help to bring you to your senses. You may be quiet and reserved, but sometimes you're like a hermit. Perhaps you exclude yourself from everyday life because you feel you don't fit in. You're learning to drop the inferiority complex and check out the facts. Your goal is to be able to connect with people on a deep level. You may seek out like-minded people with whom you feel real.

## 79/16/7

You have a strong desire to get to the top of your tree, and so you put in great effort to manifest your goals; you like to give your best to life. At times you may fear falling behind with your work or go manic trying to keep up with productivity. You're learning to relax and adopt a more philosophical view of life because it is how it is. Sometimes you take your accomplishments far too seriously. Your goal is to learn humility so you can get your life into real perspective. You enjoy innocent fun, but sometimes you know no boundaries. You're learning to be honest with yourself and become a positive role model for others.

## 88/16/7

You're dynamic and ambitious, and you're great at motivating others to use their gifts and to be successful in life. You realize that payday depends upon you delivering the goods and so you're learning to be assertive in order to stay on top of the game. At times you enjoy being the boss but you can also be ruthlessly competitive. You're learning to value teamwork as a more powerful source of growth and effectiveness. You may be spoilt materially or want to be spoon-fed. Your goal is to wake up to your spirituality and tap into your creative potential, so that you can use opportunities well.

## 97/16/7

Your aim is to please others and you're as happy as a lark as long as your skills are being put to good use. You know that everyone plays an important role influencing life, and so you're learning to set a good example. You may be frustrated when you don't reach your ideals, but like invasive thorns you tear through your fears and work even harder to achieve your dreams. Your goal is to reach enlightenment, but sometimes your intellectual understanding of the world veils you from the truth. You're learning to connect with your soul so that you can see the light, speed up your transformation and tap into your creative gifts. You're a mover and a shaker, and you simply love life.

# Name Number 8

## 17/8

You search for meaning in everyday life and you cannot rest until you find the truth. Peace of mind is important to you. If your conscience lets you know you've stepped out of bounds, you analyse your situation and go into overdrive to get yourself back on track. You're on a spiritual path where honesty and integrity rule the roost. Your goal is to find your true purpose in life. Your inflated ego and your strong intellect do sometimes stand in the way of you admitting failure in any area of your life. You're learning to wake up to reality and to focus on matters that are of importance. You tend to be lucky because your soul protects and guides you to do what's right.

## 26/8

You're smart, sophisticated and wise, and you're able to provide for yourself and find your own direction. People are impressed by your charm, power and magnetism, but they admire your inner strength even more. Sometimes you're emotional, and you may throw tantrums or mock others with your dry sense of humour; you test people to make sure they're strong. You may teach people important lessons and you're learning to become more conscious of your gift so that it can be used effectively. You're a natural provider. Whether it's love or money you generally desire to be paid back in kind. You're learning to let go of control. Your goal is to learn to empower others to take responsibility for their own lives.

## 35/8

You're constantly re-evaluating life. You enjoy learning from your mistakes or discovering qualities or gifts that you can use to help you build a brighter future. At times you're sentimental and you may grasp hold of childhood photos or you may cling onto old relationships. You can be controlling and domineering, but you're learning to stop battling with others to get what you want. Your goal is to learn to surrender stubbornness in favour of following your divine purpose in life. You're fun-loving, expressive and highly creative with words. You may adore basking in the limelight and being the centre of attention. You're learning to wake up and use your gifts fully.

## 44/8

You're incredibly determined, down to earth and realistic about life. People are naturally drawn to you when they're ready to face important issues because you deliver home truths. You're highly competent at shouldering responsibilities. Your goal is to pass on practical skills that people can utilize to help them survive in the world. You're incredibly popular and magnetic. You're able to reach out and touch the masses because you speak the same basic language – spiritual truth. Sometimes you hoard possessions and money or you're mean with yourself. You're learning to let go of material attachments so that you can keep your whole life flowing. You're seeking outer satisfaction and success, but you're fast learning that true wealth is found within yourself.

## 53/8

You're naturally engaging, and you're interested in what everyone has to say because you're fascinated by life. You project an air of knowledge and power and you're cocksure of your authority. Whilst most people find you alluring and seductive, you're learning to lighten up. You may be a natural heavyweight in business, entertainment, or in the media, but you're striving to be successful in all areas of your life. At times you're restless, unfocused and disorganized, but you're learning that you need to remember to pay your bills if you want to be provided with a service. You know there's more to life than meets the eye; your goal is to turn inwards so that it all makes perfect sense.

## 62/8

You're a communitarian, and you work hard to provide for others' needs. Whilst you may enjoy status, power and glamour, helping others brings you untold satisfaction and gives you a strong sense of purpose. You dress to impress but you also match beauty with comfort. You may be interested in the decorative arts, jewellery, fashion, design and photography. You're always on the lookout for new ideas, which you can turn into viable business opportunities, to benefit others too. Your goal is to be able to stand up on your own rather than leaning on others to prop you up financially or otherwise. You may seek a soul mate or companion to share your life with if it's on an equal footing; opening your heart to love can help your whole life to blossom.

## 71/8

Your goal is to learn to become highly productive in life so that you can manifest your dreams and ambitions. You're learning to tap into your spiritual potential in order to utilize the tools at your disposal, which are your many talents and gifts. You aim for success, but you're learning to honour the process and to trust that situations always work out for the best. You possess a pioneering spirit that leads you on both a physical and a spiritual journey in life. Sometimes you feel isolated and withdrawn, but you need quiet times in order to help you digest experiences and learn important lessons. You're bold and audacious at times, but you may not care what people think because you're just getting on with the job.

## 80/8

You're learning to grow up and take responsibility for your own life but you don't want to carry others. You may enjoy being placed high on a pedestal, particularly when you know you've worked hard to achieve recognition, but you don't take yourself too seriously. You reject the concept of master and servant because in your mind everyone has gifts and lessons to teach each other, and you enjoy learning. Your goal is to learn to re-evaluate life daily and to keep moving on so that you don't get stuck repeating the same old patterns. Life is presenting you with opportunities to bring yourself back to life – by facing reality. You may be shrouded with spiritual protection in the process.

## 89/17/8

Your goal is to find your identity, and you may engage in some serious soul searching so that you can discover who you truly are. You're willing to take a good look at yourself because you want to improve life and become a better person. You place great emphasis on the need for knowledge and education. You're also recognizing that it's only through experience that you really learn, change and grow. At times you're hung up on rules and regulations. You're learning to let go of pressurizing yourself and others to get things right, and to simply do your best. You may feel lucky to be alive, and you graciously accept the opportunities that come your way, and say 'thank you'.

## 98/17/8

Your goal is to use your gifts to benefit humanity, rather than being motivated by the desire for power, control or world domination. You may feel lost at times, because you're re-evaluating life, cutting ties with the past and formulating your identity. You're learning to let go of anxieties and to trust that in time all will be revealed and that all is well. You're charismatic and worldly, and people may listen to what you say because of your alluring voice, which conveys compassion, kindness and understanding. You're able to help people to access and utilize their creative potential. You empower them to wake up and take responsibility for their lives.

# Name Number 9

## 18/9

You're broad-minded, and you want to continue opening up your eyes to the world and digest as much information and knowledge as you can. In the past you may have been rigid or resisted change, or you may have held on tightly to control because it gave you a sense of power. You're learning to liberate yourself by being adaptable, and by embracing new ideas and opportunities in life. You enjoy being the boss, but your dislike of authority may lead you to drum up rebellion in order to overcome opposition. You're learning to welcome others' opinions, values and beliefs, and get along with everyone. You're a natural leader but your mind can be blinkered at times. Your goal is to learn to enjoy experimenting with life.

## 27/9

You're conventional, and you generally aim to do what's expected of you and stay within the rules at all times. You want to live up to your potential and so you criticize and pressurize yourself in order to get things right and gain others' approval. You may think you're not bright, attractive, or good enough, and you may view yourself through others' eyes. You're learning to accept yourself (and others), to do your best, and to develop a true sense of proportion. You enjoy all the fine things in life – champagne, caviar and vintage wines or clothes – because they make you feel at home. You're sensitive and may possess psychic skills. Your goal is to learn to refine your spirituality. You're also learning to identify and address long-term commitments.

## 36/9

Your goal is to learn to enjoy giving to others, so that life becomes a pleasure rather than a duty. You are extremely generous with your time, love and money, but you may feel disillusioned and disappointed when situations don't turn out as you expect. You deliver to your own very high standards in life but you may also demand the impossible from others. You're learning to set people free. You're sporty and active, and are also interested in the bigger issues in life: the environment, humanitarian causes, human rights, and so on. Your centre of existence is your heart because love, friendships and community are, for you, what makes life worthwhile. You want to get to the top of the tree professionally and socially. You're learning to love life as it is.

## 45/9

You're a grafter, and soul endurance ensures that you are able to carry on at life until your job is done. You're learning to keep faith and hope alive within yourself; praying may provide you with divine inspiration. You believe in yourself but sometimes life pushes your boundaries to the limit. You're learning to grasp every opportunity to learn important lessons so you can improve your life. You're constantly trying to make sense of situations. Your goal is to pass on your knowledge and wisdom so that it can uplift others. You may feel melancholy at times, particularly when material concerns and responsibilities feel so heavy. You're learning to focus on what is working. Your fundamental outlook on life is changing. Welcome spiritual transformation into your life.

## 54/9

You're an idealist, but you're also incredibly realistic about life. You're practical and loyal, and you stand by others, patiently waiting for them to finish a project or progress in life. You're extremely good at sensing what people need, and then your aim is to please. You're secretive and people may only find out by chance that you've won the lottery or moved house. You want to prove to yourself that you're capable of handling any situation in life on your own. You're learning to reach out and ask for help because you can't be superwoman or superman all the time. You possess acres of common sense, but your acute sensitivity can leave you teetering on the edge. You're learning to be factual and rationalize life.

## 63/9

Your goal is to step outside of yourself and find an important mission in life. For example, you may be a talented and successful artist whose mission it is to make art classes available for the masses. Your true mission is to live up to your potential and to serve your soul by using your gifts to inspire and uplift others. You possess a passion for life. You're loving, generous and extremely creative. Sometimes people may feel overpowered or overshadowed by your greatness and enthusiasm. You're learning to recognize there's a time and space for everything. You respect others' gifts and enjoy cultural diversity because it enriches life.

### 72/9

You're sensitive and intuitive, and you like working with facts. You can be brutally honest with others; you harmlessly adopt this tack to help them break down their illusions. You may be a natural healer who constantly gives to others, but your goal is to allow space for your own healing process too. Perhaps you spend much time meditating, soul searching, or studying subjects that help you to reflect, let go and move on in life. You're fastidious about cleanliness and fussy over appearances, but rather than judging what's on the cover you're learning to go for what's real. You're interested in cutting-edge documentaries. Your goal is to be a leader in your field.

### 81/9

You're ambitious and driven to succeed. Perhaps you may be sought after as a guru in your field of expertise. You may feel like one of the privileged few. You seem to amass many honours and trophies in your lifetime without even trying; you show humility. At times you may feel weary with life because you've seen it all and done it all before. You're learning to rekindle your passion by reconnecting to your spirituality, by meditating, going on a retreat or by getting together with like-minded people. Your goal is to get organized and wake up to your responsibilities. You're an inspiration to others.

## 90/9

You're a high achiever, but you tend to work best under pressure or when there's a collective need. You're one of life's little helpers but you're learning to allow yourself to be lazy and 'slack off' once in a while. You possess strong views on life, but at times you self-righteously preach on at others or you act like you 'know it all'. You're learning to forgive so that you can forget the past, and also to accept others. Whilst your goal is to attain knowledge, you do accept that experience is the best teacher in life. You are deeply in contact with your soul and you allow your inner wisdom to be the guiding force in your life.

## 99/18/9

You may possess an abundance of money, power or possessions, but you spread your wealth around by offering people opportunities to climb on board. You may be only too willing to give away all your worldly wares if it makes people happy or provides for their needs. Whilst you're a guide for others and your wisdom comes free of charge, you're learning to be more astute financially. Your goal is to learn to let go of all that you know, so that you can rejuvenate and transform your life. You may be highly sexed, and also passionate about your hobbies and interests. Your charm, magnetism and powerful presence ensure that you're always blessed with good company. You get along with everyone.

Chapter 7

# Public Names

## Harnessing Creative Potential

H ave you been inspired by people's talents or ever pondered long and hard on where your child got some of their incredible gifts? All your creative potential is contained within the numbers from your overall birth chart (full birth names and date of birth). However, in order to be able to harness your gifts effectively you first need to be able to recognize what qualities and potential are available to you. *Choose the Perfect Baby Name* can help you to recognize key qualities, gifts and positive potential contained within all babies' names.

Some children tap into their creative potential at an early age. For example, Michael Jackson knew when he was in infancy that he wanted to be a singer and entertainer. He then followed this through with action, love and dedication in order to become a global superstar and to use his gifts. Some children demonstrate their gifts immediately, like those with Mensa brains, who are born recognizing their potential genius. For example, they may become breathtaking chess players, mathematicians, or scientists and these children are content simply to get on with the job they have come here to do.

There is always more potential available than you can use, which is why so many famous people are able to reinvent themselves. For example, heartthrob actor George Clooney uses his fame to draw attention to his other passion, humanitarian causes, and he is a seriously powerful human rights campaigner. Madonna is always changing the flavour of her music and dress style and has forged a successful career that's already lasted decades.

Famous people have Public Names that you are able to recognize instantly because they have become household names. It's been said that the most famous of people on the planet are recognized simply by their First Names. For example, everyone knows who Kylie, Elton and Angelina are! Other 'Public Names' are recognizable by their Family Name only, for example, Obama, Mandela, Beckham. This indicates the specific gifts they're recognized for may be coming from their genetic Family Name. The Dalai Lama or Chancellor Merkel, are potent Stage Names too. DVB is the Brand Name for Victoria and David Beckham, and Virgin is one of many Brand Names used by entrepreneur Richard Branson. Stage Names and Brand Names can also help you to explore your creative potential fully.

Here are some fascinating people with Public Names who were or are able to tap into their creative potential successfully.

# FLORENCE NIGHTINGALE Birth Names
# 'THE LADY WITH THE LAMP' Pet Name

Florence was a pioneering English nurse who walked the ward rounds at night in the hospital where she worked. She always carried a lamp so the sick and injured called her by the Pet Name, 'The Lady With The Lamp'. She was also a writer and a statistician.

- *Achievements*: Pioneered nursing standards, which stand to this day. 'International Nurses Day' is celebrated on her birthday.
- *First Name*: Florence, 42/6. Potential: loyalty, compassion, ability to provide practical and emotional support to others.
- *Family Name*: Nightingale, 61/7. Potential: productivity, love of community, truth.
- *Expression Number*: Florence Nightingale, 103/13/4. Potential: to wake up to responsibilities, ability to facilitate others' spiritual growth and transformation, communication skills.
- *Pet Name*: The Lady With The Lamp, 84/12/3. Potential: hands-on helper, multi-tasking, ability to shoulder many responsibilities, organized, ability to finish what has been started.

Did Florence use her potential? Yes, her various names enabled her to tap into care and compassion; physical endurance helped her as a nurse. Her Pet Name Number 3 helped her to tap into her communication and writing skills.

# DONALD TRUMP

**Stage Name and Birth Names (born Donald John Trump)**

Donald is an extraordinarily successful American business-man and property developer; he's also an author, socialite and television personality. He is the father of five children.

- *Achievements*: business – too many to list!
- First Name: Donald, 23/5. Potential: communication, ability to make sense of life, adventure, self-expression, popularity, knowledgeable.
- *Family Name*: Trump, 25/7. Potential: direct communication, trust, nature-loving, analytical, mover and shaker, ability to make things happen.
- *Overall Stage Names*: Donald Trump, 48/12/3. Potential: ability to complete contracts, inner strength, business flair, humour, efficiency, self-expression.

Is Donald living up to his potential? Yes, his Stage Names (Birth Names) are supporting him to use his communication and business skills and to express himself fully.

# DIANA, PRINCESS OF WALES

**Stage Name (born The Honourable Diana Frances Spencer)**

Diana was born into English nobility, and she loved singing, dancing, sports and caring for children – for a short while she became a professional nanny. She experienced a fairytale wedding to Prince Charles; she then bore two heirs before divorcing. She devoted her latter life to charity work, and uplifted people with her natural charm, affection and playful sense of humour.

- *Achievements*: The Diana Memorial Award;, supported and campaigned for numerous charities around the world.
- *Overall Stage Names*: Diana, Princess of Wales, 87/16/7. Potential: introspection, truth, power and status, personal development, ability to instigate change, intuition.

Did she achieve her potential in her lifetime? Yes, because this title gave her the power and status to be able to instigate positive change with regards to humanitarian issues and her various charities. Diana was not able to explore more of her full potential because she died at the age of 36.

# ELTON JOHN

**Stage Name (born Reginald Kenneth Dwight)**

Elton is an outstanding singer-songwriter and musician, and he devotes much time to fund-raising for his charity. He married his long-time lover David Furnish.

- *Achievements*: CBE. Sold over 250 million records. Formed The Elton John Aids Foundation.
- *First Name*: Elton, 21/3. Potential: self-expression, inspiration, creativity, good at multi-tasking, entertaining, humorous, active.
- *Family Name*: John, 20/2. Potential: wisdom, love, kindness, protection, ability to make decisions, intuition.
- *Overall Stage Names*: Elton John, 41/5. Potential: abundance, adventure, communication, knowledge, ambition, physical endurance, popularity, spontaneity.

Is Elton fulfilling his creative potential? Yes, his Stage Name has helped him enormously to communicate and express himself through his music and through the field of entertainment. It has also helped to expand his love and compassion out to the world through his charity work.

# ANTONY (born Marcus Antonius) and CLEOPATRA
## (born Cleopatra VII Philopator) Stage Name Together

Antony and Cleopatra were famous lovers, who produced three children together.

- *Achievements*: Cleopatra was the last ruler of Egypt before it was named a Roman Province. Antony was a military commander and administrator, and cousin of Julius Caesar.
- *Overall*: Independently they both achieved power and status.
- *First Name*: Antony, 26/8. Potential: inner strength, ambition, wisdom, love, compassion, status, power, authority, charm, wake up to responsibilities.
- *First Name*: Cleopatra, 35/8. Potential: inner strength, reflection, self-expression, ambition, making sense of life, creative, adventurous, magnetic, powerful, wake-up call to responsibilities.
- *Overall Stage Name together*: Antony (26) + Cleopatra (35), 61/7. Potential: spiritual connection, soul searching, love, beauty, wisdom, manifestation, fertility of ideas, productivity, trust, truth.

Did they fulfil their potential together? Yes and no. They were both strong characters that held positions of power and status, and they were magnetically drawn together. They experienced a deep soul connection and were powerful mirrors for each other to be able to see the truth. Had they lived longer, it's likely their relationship would have developed to deeper levels of love and commitment and they may have shared a long-lasting journey of self-development together.

# BILL AND HILLARY CLINTON

**Stage Names, Birth Names and Marriage Name**

Bill and Hillary are American politicians, humanitarians, environmental campaigners, and powerful leaders in their field. They have one daughter, Chelsea.

- *Achievements*: Hillary is a lawyer and currently the 67th American Secretary Of State. Bill Clinton was President of the United States, and set up the William J. Clinton Foundation, including the Clinton Haiti Fund.
- *First Name*: Bill, 17/8. Potential: spiritual protection, ambition, inner strength, empowerment, wake up spiritually, organization, status, power.
- *First Name*: Hillary, 40/4. Potential: loyal, passionate, down to earth, reliable, ability to implement new structures, physical endurance.
- *Family Name*: Clinton, 33/6. Potential: service to the family and community, love, wisdom, compassion, inspiration, devotion, sacrifice.
- *Overall Stage Name together*: Bill (17) + Hillary (40) + Clinton (33), 90/9. Potential: guides, teachers, worldly and wise, knowledge, education, passion, inclusiveness.

Are they fulfilling their potential together? Yes, because they are helping each other to fulfil their own destiny and empowering each other to be the best they can, whilst focusing on the bigger picture.

# DAVID BECKHAM

**Stage Name and Birth Names (born David Robert Joseph Beckham)**

David is an English footballer, hero to many children around the world. He is also a highly successful model, fashion icon and businessman. He married famous singer, model and designer Victoria Beckham and she bore three boys.

- *Achievements*: Received over 100 caps playing for England. Founded The David Beckham Academy. Founded DVB business brand (with his wife Victoria).
- *First Name*: David, 22/4. Potential: ability to lay foundations for others, sensitivity, wisdom, hard worker, down to earth, loyal, reliable.
- *Family Name*: Beckham, 25/7, potential: deep thinker, analytical, sensitive, direct, ability to manifest dreams and goals, productivity.
- *Stage Name*: David Beckham, 49/13/4. Potential: spiritual growth, self-expression, adaptability, learning and education, ability to make a difference to the world, passionate.

Is David using his full Stage Name potential? Yes, but there's still so much more for him to achieve. This Stage Name is helping David to push beyond his boundaries and utilize his creative skills in the fields of business and education.

Part Two

# Popular
# Baby Names

Chapter 8

# 100 Popular Baby Names

Numerology enables you to tap into the sounds that each name makes so that you can connect with its essence, and gain clarity by accessing the deeper meaning it conveys. In this chapter you can read key traits for 100 popular baby names from various cultures. Each name has been transcribed into numbers from the alphabet (read Chapter 3, 'How to Transcribe Names into Numbers and Draw Up a Birth Chart'). You will notice that some boys' and girls' names add up to the same larger numbers. For example, Ethan and Mary both add up to 21. However, the descriptions are very different because they're made up from a different sequence of numbers, which changes their meaning and potential. You can 'read' names in many different ways but your intuition is the best guide.

Chapter 6, 'Fine-Tuning the Name Numbers', focuses on the fine-tuning of the single-digit numbers 1 to 9. For example, Mariah adds up to 32 (3+2=5); you can look up the larger number 32/5 in that section of the chapter. It is, however, always the single-digit numbers that are the most potent. So for Mariah it's a 5 that exerts the most influence, but both the 3 and 2 offer finer-tuned influences that help to refine and clarify the 5 vibration. You can read about the true essence of any name number 1 to 9 in Chapter 4, 'Names Decoded'.

It's fascinating to see that the most popular baby names are the same the world over. For example, John always appears in Most Popular lists, but with a slightly different spelling: Johan, Jon, Jonathan, Jonas, and so on. The spelling of the name brings different influences based upon the consciousness of the country or culture it represents, but we are all one.

# 50 Popular Boys' Names

## ADAM
### 1 4 1 4 = 10/1

You're thirsty for knowledge, and you're restless to feed your brain with constant new information. Perhaps you eat your breakfast whilst checking over emails and reading the newspaper, or you study for two degrees at once. You love change but unexpected events can catapult you out of your comfort zone, but at least this keeps you on your toes. You're sexually magnetic, but people are drawn to your fascinating mind in equal measure. You may be drawn into addictions, but you're learning to use your mind to access your inner wisdom that can help you on your journey. You're learning to share your knowledge with others and to use your creativity.

## AIDEN
### 1 9 4 5 5 = 24/6

You like to surround yourself with family and friends and you find safety in numbers. You often work with colleagues on team projects because it makes you feel happy. Your aim is to create a comfortable lifestyle for yourself and others; you're likely to be cosseted and spoiled by loved ones too. Sulking is your medium of attention, but if you're left alone the moment passes and life eventually resumes back to normal. You may be traditional in your attitude to relationships. Sometimes you seek out glitz and glamour; great as long as you realize it's real life and real people that really count.

## ALEXANDER
1 3 5 6 1 5 4 5 9 = 39/12/3

You like to start things but can forget to finish them off. Perhaps because you leave things to the last minute or keep too many pots on the boil at once. You're incredibly entertaining with a great sense of humour, and you appear worldly. You seek approval and aim to attain distinction with all your pursuits in life. You're incredibly unfocused at times or too laid back in your attitude to important issues, until you recognize what you're doing. You're good at taking action. You're a hands-on helper, tactile and warm, but you're also a social and political animal too.

## ALFIE
1 3 6 9 5 = 24/6

Ideally you want everyone to be friends and get along with each other, and you aim to create a safe network of nice people around you. Life can be painful when you discover that reality is often very different from your dreams. You see the best in people and bring your love and warmth into situations that need healing. You possess a jealous streak. You're learning to value your own strengths and recognize your inner beauty rather than focusing on what you're not or haven't got. You're earthy and practical, and you're brilliant at organizing and managing a team.

# ANDREW
## 1 5 4 9 5 5 = 29/11/2

You're passionate about life. Your fear of failure forces you to put in strenuous effort to ensure your goals succeed. Like a new soul you keep on trying; each time you wake up to more of your potential you give yourself even more goals to achieve. You constantly strive to follow your aspirations. There is a fine balancing act between fulfilling your desires and your needs, but this process feels easier if you keep your eye on the bigger picture. You can always call upon your strong sense of rationale to straighten out your nerves or emotions.

# ANTHONY
## 1 5 2 8 6 5 7 = 34/7

You're learning to become more self-conscious, so that you can improve yourself and your life. You may enjoy meditation, reading thought-provoking books, or attending lectures that enlighten you on world issues. Perhaps you may simply start to notice the trail of clues that life presents to you on your journey. At times you prefer to remain innocent and naïve or to be kept in the dark about reality so that you can safely stay involved in your own little world. Reality bites; all is well as long as you learn to be honest with yourself and about what you want in life.

# BENJAMIN
2 5 5 1 1 4 9 5 = 32/5

You love travelling, music, dancing and using your brain; you're drawn to crosswords and puzzles for relaxation. You're naturally inquisitive but you get frustrated if you don't receive the right answers to your questions. You're gentle and placid, and enjoy quiet time reading, meditating and studying. You need your own space and become agitated or defensive if you aren't able to create 'me time'. Sometimes you simply disappear out the door and are incredibly secretive about your whereabouts; you enjoy your freedom. You are learning to develop your sense of self-esteem so that you can shine, and also to communicate who you are to the world.

# BLAKE
2 3 1 2 5 = 13/4

You're uplifted by your mind and imagination, but you also possess a black-and-white attitude towards life. You're learning to merge your soul and personality into one so that you can enjoy expansion in all areas of your life. You're childlike and fun, and you enjoy the simple pleasures in life. You're learning to take responsibility for your material needs. You may feel disturbed by moving house or even by eating different foods; it's important to keep expressing your feelings. Paradoxically, people may be surprised or shocked by the 'out-of-the-blue' dramatic changes you make. Spiritual growth is your main goal in life.

# CHARLIE
## 3 8 1 9 3 9 5 = 38/11/2

You may attract fame and recognition due to your inspirational creative gifts. You may offer a high level of service in your field. The flip side of fame is notoriety and people may associate you with either. Whilst both can at times be empty experiences, they can teach you about what's important in life – love and truth. You aim to lead a simple life but power, money and success turn you on. You may carry too many responsibilities. You love rescuing the broken-hearted, but you're learning to take good care of yourself too. You're growing up and are able to listen to wisdom. You're shrewd in business.

# CHRISTIAN
## 3 8 9 9 1 2 9 1 5 = 47/11/2

You have many dreams for yourself and the world, and you're good at spreading the message so that others can join forces to turn their dreams into reality. You can be forceful and you're learning the art of patience. You're a powerful leader because you're prepared to seek out those who can help you fill in another piece of the jigsaw in order to get the job done. You're a busy bee but you're learning to focus all your energies on what you're doing at the time so as to avoid unnecessary slip-ups. You're learning to relate on an emotional level so that you can feel closer to people.

# CHRISTOPHER
3 8 9 9 1 2 6 7 8 5 9  = 67/13/4

You experience abundance in your life and you're learning to appreciate how lucky you are to be given all your chances in life. Sometimes burdens get you down, but not for long because you can always see the bigger picture; answers come to you. You are prepared to walk a long way for your friends, but you can be black and white and easily feel betrayed. You are able to muster up all your worth in order to forgive and forget others' mistakes, after all no-one's perfect. You're embarking upon a lifetime of personal or soul development. At times you may want a donkey to carry your load, but external wake-up calls jolt you awake and urge you to take responsibility for your life, which you can do. You're a powerful healer.

# CONNOR
3 6 5 5 6 9  = 34/7

People may be fooled by your easy-going nature, but you're so focused on your goals behind the scenes. It can surprise others when you come up trumps. A part of you may well be happy escaping to some exotic geographical location and living the easy life. You're observant and sensitive to people's moods, and you may put on an act simply to lift them up and give them what they need. You create solid friendships and you stay true to those you love for life. You love fooling around and entertaining others.

## COOPER
3 6 6 7 5 9 = 36/9

You're wise beyond your years, and you expect those around you to understand your ways. You'd like to change the world, but first you recognize your need to educate yourself on important matters. You spend time in class learning, absorbing information on the web, or watching documentaries. You're also learning how best to express yourself and your beliefs, in a way that people warm to and respect. You can be obsessive about issues or get so drawn into arguments and debates that you lose the objective. You're generally kind and respectful towards others, and your silly sense of humour is endearing and helps to lighten their mood during critical times. People either like you or tolerate you, but you're larger than life and you certainly make your mark.

## DANIEL
4 1 5 9 5 3 = 27/9

You're a long-term planner, and you aim to take on only those commitments that you truly know you can keep. Paradoxically, people find you incredibly challenging to pin down because you're so secretive about your intentions. You're accomplished at changing the subject or disappearing during crucial moments in a conversation. You seek out knowledge but may dislike learning from others; you like to think you know it all. You may feel superior but life is teaching you humility. You're capable of great things and you're learning to work hard and manifest your goals a step at a time, and with great determination.

# DAVID
## 4 1 4 9 4  = 22/4

Once you've learned to keep your feet on the ground, you may actually enjoy being shaken and stirred so that life remains a constant source of stimulation. You're very capable, and you take the attitude that it's up to you to create your own empire. You may see problems as challenges that help you to overcome your own limitations. You learn so much by taking the bigger view of life. At times you're capable of turning an oasis into a sandstorm, but by learning to see situations for what they are you may avoid dramas and provide yourself with opportunities for spiritual growth. You're learning to keep life simple and to embrace change.

# DYLAN
## 4 7 3 1 5  = 20/2

You're a bit of a dreamer, and you love building castles in your mind where everything's possible. However, you're also great at manifesting your dreams; all that daydreaming enables you to obtain clarity about what you want and then you follow your vision. You're open to life, but you can be overprotective about your ideas. You're learning to share your life with others and help them to manifest their desires too. You possess strong survival instincts and can be highly protective. You're learning to be wise and fair in all your dealings.

# ETHAN
## 5 2 8 1 5 = 21/3

You're fun-loving and ambitious, and you like to get your own way, which can be complicated because life isn't all about you. You're inspirational, and capable of producing great moments of genius because your mind is able to reach out to new ideas and you follow them through. You're generally easy-going but sometimes you withdraw into your mind for protection when life gets too much; see these times as an investment as they enable you to regroup. Some people may regard you as light-weight, but you're a deep thinker and often surprise others with your incredible observations on life.

# FINLAY
## 6 9 5 3 1 7 = 31/4

You're team-orientated and are happy to speak up for others' rights, but sometimes you need to accept life's limitations. You possess a sentimental streak; you hold on to old photos and letters in your memory box for life. You're hard-working and practical with business affairs, and you like to keep your house in order. It's love that holds your world together and truth that matters, so your goal is to find work that delivers inner growth in addition to material security. You enjoy working through obstacles and stretching your abilities to the max because it brings you a greater sense of achievement.

# GABRIEL
7 1 2 9 9 5 3 = 36/9

Your primary motivation is to help people in any way you can. You're learning to be generous with your love and time, but in a way that includes your own needs being met too because you may neglect yourself. You see life as a learning experience. You aim to improve life for others by using your business or teaching skills or by using your creativity. You are soul-centred and whilst there are times when you can be selfish, superior or superficial, you generally look inwards for guidance and inspiration. You're learning to constantly adapt to change and keep growing. There is no rest for the good.

# GEORGE
7 5 6 9 7 5 = 39/12/3

You're adaptable and you generally make the most of what life delivers to your doorstep. Whilst most people need organization to structure their day, the more chaotic life becomes the more you seem to accomplish. This may be due to your fast brain that ticks away and computes various formulas for events and situations; you're able to spring into systematic action. Your multi-tasking abilities are breathtaking. You are at your best when helping others. You can be harshly critical of your own accomplishments even when you've done well, and done your best. You're learning to be kind to yourself.

## HARRY
8 1 9 9 7 = 34/7

You're a happy-go-lucky person, and you possess a strong sense of knowing what's right. You can be materialistic, self-preoccupied or feel detached from the world at times. You can be evasive and, like an ostrich, refuse to budge or accept reality. You're learning to recognize your strengths and challenges, and to express gratitude for your lot. You possess leadership abilities, which deter you from drifting aimlessly through life. If you want something you realize you need to apply yourself and make your goals happen, which you aim to do. You like telling jokes and you're learning to live lightly on planet earth.

## HARVEY
8 1 9 4 5 7 = 34/7

You're down to earth, creative and analytical. You can see right through people, and you can instinctively feel whether they are genuine or not. You can be stubborn and wilful. You're your own boss and you refuse to be dictated to; you want people to follow your lead. You enjoy power by becoming the authority on a subject or in a profession. You're learning to lighten up and take yourself less seriously. You are able to successfully juggle responsibilities. You're learning to remember to exercise and also to socialize in order to let your hair down, relax and have some fun.

# IVAN
## 9 4 1 5  = 19=10=1

You want to achieve distinction in life and you want to prove to the world that you're the best. Over a lifetime your firmly held beliefs can dramatically change. You're learning to stop judging yourself and let go of your need to collect certificates or medals to prove you're a decent and respectable human being. As long as you accept who you are and approve of yourself, that's what matters. You may seek permission from your parents or friends whom you place in authority to do what you need to do, but you're learning to courageously follow your own path in life regardless. You're unique.

# JACK
## 1 1 3 2  = 7

You're a little ray of sunshine and you're able to lift people up and inspire truth within them. You enjoy the simple life, and value quiet times alone or with loved ones where you can be yourself. You're a great communicator because you're so perceptive, and you have a knack of knowing exactly when and what needs to be said. You're a nature lover at heart. Whilst you possess high expectations of others, your kind are able to forgive easily. You're learning to live in accordance with spiritual truth. You may meditate and introspect to access your higher self and connect with your soul.

## JACOB
1 1 3 6 2 = 13/4

You're being shown enormous opportunities for spiritual growth. This can help to catapult you forwards and enrich all areas of your life, and it's good to remember this if you find yourself stuck in a rut. You're self-reliant and responsible, and you like to devote your time to important issues of the day. You want to make a tangible difference in life and build a better world for everyone. You're constantly making things with your hands. It's good to learn to keep talking and keep expressing yourself fully because it can help to boost your self-confidence. You're learning to believe in yourself.

## JAKE
1 1 2 5 = 9

Jake adds up to a 9, which contains all the energies of the numbers 1 to 9 within it. You may be humble, worldly and wise, and people may come to you for spiritual guidance and healing. People may even put you on a pedestal, but you're learning to respect that everyone's equal and to rejoice when others use their gifts and shine. You're a trailblazer about important issues and you're willing to speak your truth if you think it can create positive change. You're sometimes emotionally unstable, but your strong spiritual connection grounds you right back into reality. You experience deep emotions, which enable you to relate and reach out to others.

## JAMES
1 1 4 5 1  = 12/3

You're like a little teddy bear, providing comfort and cuddles to those who need to feel loved and wanted. You're incredibly versatile with your talents. You're prepared to get your hands dirty because you love giving. You get along with people and generally do what's required. You're observant and you can see right through people and situations. You're a natural counsellor. Sometimes you enjoy partying too much and get yourself into all kinds of sticky situations. You enjoy seeing people eat the cakes you've baked. You truly care about the world and want to do things that you know will be of use.

## JAYDEN
1 1 7 4 5 5  = 23/5

Your mission in life is to master the art of communication: telepathy, body language, sex, music, dancing, writing, talking, right through to deep inner communication with your soul. You love life, and may enjoy living on the edge, but you're learning to adopt common sense and also to use your creativity. You're sometimes intense to be around as you're supercharged with nervous energy, but your uncanny ability to read people gives you valuable clues to what you need to do. You lead a colourful life. You love learning and the richness of knowledge helps you along your way.

# JOHN
## 1 6 8 5 = 20/2

You're quietly spoken but you possess such a clear way with words that you instantly grab people's attention and they get the meaning. You're sensitive and vulnerable emotionally, which are wonderful qualities to explore with your soul mate. You're learning to choose carefully when and with whom you bare your soul. At times when you're feeling defenceless you may 'fight' like a cat, and your raw emotions produce dramatic words that wound people. Learning to heal your emotions can help you feel more comfortable with yourself and others. Your inner wisdom is always there to guide and support you.

# JOSEPH
## 1 6 1 5 7 8 = 28/10/1

You're very directional, and a born leader, but at times you allow your emotions to get in the way of success. This is because you're constantly trying to make sense of situations and weighing up whether you're doing the right thing. Procrastination is a productivity killer. If you listen to your soul and abide by your conscience, you can be clear about what you need to do; knowing why you need to do something can also help you to make your next move. Regular exercise can help you release pentup emotions and you're learning to channel your creative energies positively.

# JOSHUA
## 1 6 1 8 3 1  = 20/2

Harmony is your aim, and you want to spread the good news of one world, one life, and one love. You're extremely sensitive and thoughtful, and you carry yourself through life in a very caring manner. You can instantly feel what people need or want, and you're quick to defend or protect loved ones, to the extent you'll 'fight'. You love yoga and swimming, and make time to listen to others. You're shrewd in business and are happy to push for promotion if it means extra riches, which you share with others. You respect your intuition and your inner wisdom.

# LACHLAN
## 3 1 3 8 3 1 5  = 24/6

You possess many diverse interests in life, and whilst time is a gift it also proves to be a challenge when you're trying to pack everything in. You sometimes worry that you'll reach those pearly gates only to find your goals have been left far behind. You barely sleep once you're on track, but your relentless determination pays off and produces results in every area of your life. You desire a harmonious life filled with love and laughter, community and creative work. You're learning to be practical and realize that life isn't perfect, and also to continue giving all your love and support to those in need.

# LIAM
## 3 9 1 4 = 17/8

Your life is filled with purpose and direction, and your intuition is guiding you along a path that's laden with powerful lessons and experiences. It's time to grow up and take full responsibility for your words and actions. You're learning to think carefully before you speak. You're stubborn and sometimes your 'couldn't-care-less' attitude may cause chaos around you. You're humble enough to learn from your mistakes and you are blatantly direct with people about your true feelings. You're a pioneer, and are incredibly inventive with new ideas. You aim to execute a strategy that guarantees success. You tend to be lucky in life.

# LOGAN
## 3 6 7 1 5 = 22/4

You're great at judging what needs to be done next on the agenda. You may possess a reputation as the one who knows. You thrive off practical knowledge and savour reading about ways you can improve upon your lifestyle: books on DIY, Feng Shui, design or architecture. You possess strong beliefs about how you think things should be done, but at the end of the day you are willing to take the group consensus. You're a person of routine, and you can resist change by digging in your heels and refusing to budge, but life always finds a way to put you straight back into the potential.

# LUCAS
## 3 3 3 1 1  = 11/2

You use your wisdom to help others; perhaps you become a doctor or a vet or work with children; whatever career path you choose your vocation is service. You may find yourself listening to others' problems and saying a few words or telling a joke to lift people out of their situations or suffering. You recognize that the whole world needs healing. You feel used at times, but because you're so kind and generous with your love and support you keep on giving. You love to love, but your high expectations can create emotional turmoil in your life until you learn to adapt to reality.

# MATTHEW
## 4 1 2 2 8 5 5  = 27/9

You may come across as a tough cookie but you're incredibly soft inside, and you're kind and giving. You're a deep thinker with interests in the arts, philosophy, psychology, spirituality and religion. It's important for you to keep up with current affairs as it helps you feel connected to life. You're great at networking and you love to organize parties, political debates and get-togethers where you can highlight good causes and raise awareness. You seek security but you seek out those who inspire you in life. You can be protective about your privacy, but you're learning to open up and reveal your true self.

# MAX
## 4  1  6  = 11/2

You know how to use every available resource and how to put them to good use; they help you to accomplish your mission in life. You enjoy abundance but focusing all your energy on worldly gains may leave you feeling isolated and empty. You're learning to be productive by co-creating with others, by finding your teammate in business, your soul mate in love, and then by creating even more success together. You're refining your spirituality, and you're motivated to serve and help others. Sometimes you can be temperamental and edgy because you're unsure of yourself, but learning to focus on the job at hand can help your fears to simply fade away.

# MICHAEL
## 4  9  3  8  1  5  3  = 33/6

You'd give your last loaf of bread to a neighbour in need, and your ability to make sacrifices for family, friends and community is touching. You see the best in people but you may sometimes take it to heart when life seems different to how it appears on the surface. You're abundantly creative and you love to paint, cook, write, and also look after others' needs. You tend to neglect yourself, so developing a selfish streak by saying 'no' to others' demands occasionally is real mastery. You are able to access deep-seated emotions which bubble to the surface, and you quickly pick up on others' feelings too. You surround yourself with a loving and strong network of friends for mutual support.

# MOHAMMED
4 6 8 1 4 4 5 4  = 36/9

You possess strong opinions and you put your beliefs into action and demonstrate your values. For example, you may value respect and so you set a good example by being respectful towards everyone you meet. You create a secure network of friends and family around you. You're passionate that everyone within your community should pull their weight. You work hard to build financial stability but you're learning to take only what you need. You enjoy living in the present. You love life when you're able to be creative and express your love and wisdom to the world.

# NATHAN
5 1 2 8 1 5  = 22/4

You're strong-willed, which helps you to focus and achieve your goals. You're a warrior for peace, and you're learning to lay down strong roots that others can build upon for the future. You're interested in facts and figures and possess a scientific brain that questions everything. Sometimes common sense flies out of the window due to your powerful emotions, which overpower your logic. You're learning to reassure yourself that you're loved and wanted. You may procrastinate over inconsequential issues, but once you feel safe you go for life full on. You're a stabilizing force in others' lives.

# NICHOLAS
## 5 9 3 8 6 3 1 1 = 36/9

You're truly a compassionate person, but you don't suffer fools gladly. Those who refuse to take responsibility for their lives irritate you. You are broad-minded but you possess a rebellious streak and a bloody-minded attitude towards others who dare to tell you what to do or think. You always think you're right but you're learning to ask for help from others also in the know. You're pushy with situations that need moving on, and then you may feel as though you're on a mission to save the world. You've a gift with words and may be interested in journalism, writing books, teaching and education, or human rights.

# NOAH
## 5 6 1 8 = 20/2

How long can you hang on to a boat if it's sinking? The answer is to learn to let go of control and to accept that change happens every moment of every day. You're spinning around inspired by the inner beauty of life, but you're learning to keep calm and carry on. As long as you feel loved then you're happy, and you want to please others. You emit a sense of serene inner wisdom and are a port for others in their emotional storms because you're a great listener. Sometimes you suffocate others by being emotionally demanding. You may want your desires to fall into your lap effortlessly. You're letting go of manipulation and learning the art of compromise.

# OLIVER
## 6 3 9 4 5 9  = 36/9

You love animals, children, and the elderly, and you thrive on caring for family and community. You can earn your own living but sometimes feeding the 'five thousand' is hard; it's only sheer determination that carries you through. You're cultural, and your mind contains an encyclopaedia of general knowledge. Photography, the arts and cooking may inspire you. You're fiery and passionate and are the driving force behind many projects, people and ideas. You're learning to keep your emotions in check by focusing on facts. Creative visualization may help you to achieve personal and collective goals.

# PETER
## 7 5 2 5 9  = 28/10/1

You're incredibly charming and sexually magnetic; part of the attraction is your aloof detachment, which conveys an air of mystery. People try to get to know the real you, but you only share your personal and intimate life with the chosen few. You are bullish and are determined to achieve your goals no matter what, but you can appear fearsome at times. You possess an air of innocence and naïvety even though you may achieve great highs in your life (particularly in your career). You can be materialistic. You're learning to grow up and find your own direction in life.

# RILEY
## 9 9 3 5 7 = 33/6

You're at your happiest when you're utilizing your abundant creativity, and when you have the freedom to express yourself fully. You like to work and socialize in groups. This helps you to build self-confidence as you merge into one, and lose yourself in the process of achieving team goals. You do enjoy being the centre of attention, generally for all the right reasons. You're dedicated to a cause, but you can be taken in by the promise of glamour, romance or goodies at the end of the rainbow. You're learning to read the small print before signing away your soul.

# ROBERT
## 9 6 2 5 9 2 = 33/6

You're a good person at heart, and your loved ones take priority over the rest of your life. Sometimes you can be thoughtless, selfish and deliberately forgetful towards others' needs; but you're learning to treat people with respect. You go deeply into relationships and friendships, but you find it a challenge to let go. You hold on in case there is anything more to learn or perhaps because you want to protect yourself from getting hurt. You're learning to see the wisdom in situations so that you can build honest friendships. You're good at making things with your hands, but you're a visual person and you may be passionate about the arts or photography.

# RYAN
## 9 7 1 5  = 22/4

You're happiest when you're 'holding hands' with a friend or colleague, and you're able to make a valuable contribution to the world together. Of course you know you need to take responsibility for yourself but you can achieve even more when you join forces with others. Sometimes a fear of rejection means you hold on to your emotions, where they fester and gather force only to be released when a situation provokes. By applying endurance and determination you can break through from the deep freeze of inertia. You're in charge of your own life and it's up to you to go for what you want.

# SIMON
## 1 9 4 6 5  = 25/7

You're a visionary, but you may think that only your opinions count, and naturally believe that others should fall into line. You possess unrivalled faith in yourself and your abilities, but you can listen to reason. You're analytical and perceptive, but your fussiness over details can be destructive and may result in you missing your target. You may appear cold and calculating at times, but to you life is simple – truth is the truth. You're learning to become more aware of others' feelings. You're a hands-on helper, and your desire to create a healthy lifestyle for your loved ones is inspiring.

# THOMAS
**2 8 6 4 1 1  = 22/4**

You may feel a strong emotional bond with the females in your life, because you are a gentle and intuitive soul and you seek out warmth and security. You're down to earth and possess a powerful work ethic; you beaver away until you attain your goals. You also enjoy the structure and direction that your masculine side provides. You're learning to feel comfortable with your masculine and feminine energies so that you can feel at one with yourself and life. Ultimately it's your soul that guides you; you're learning to listen and take responsibility for all that you create.

# WILLIAM
**5 9 3 3 9 1 4  = 34/7**

You prefer to let life happen and see what occurs rather than impose your will upon others or upon your destiny in life. Indeed, you're a happy-go-lucky soul, who is learning to be practical, responsible, and to get along with others in order to achieve your goals. You can be powerfully perceptive and intuitive, which you're learning to trust. Deep down you're a family- and community-orientated person. You can also learn to let go of selfishness or self-preoccupation in order to create loving relationships and receive all the care you deserve.

# 50 Popular Girls' Names

## ABIGAIL
1 2 9 7 1 9 3  = 32/5

You are amusing, and you're able to colourfully narrate stories that bring a deeper meaning to people's lives. You're entertaining, and some may say eccentric, but you're happy as long as you're free to be. You're gifted with words and languages, and may be drawn to writing, teaching and art. You're a hands-on carer but you tend to only stop when you drop; you're learning to be sensible about your needs. You're very open with your friends and willingly accept their failings. You may find it challenging to commit in relationships. You're learning to examine your emotions so that you can heal the past and take some risks in love and life.

## ADDISON
1 4 4 9 1 6 5  = 30/3

You're learning to target your words carefully because you know that when you speak without thinking it gets you into trouble, as it has, and you want to change. You're sporty and energetic, and you love the idea of jogging through life with the wind in your hair and hardly a care in the world. You analyse your performance repeatedly, and set yourself goals to do better (in all areas of your life). You enjoy playing sports because it brings a social dynamic and it helps you to chill out. You enjoy observing people so you can pick up tips; life is great as long as you're learning.

# ALEXIS
## 1 3 5 6 9 1 = 25/7

You want to stay in control of your life and situations, but the more you try to arrange situations the more life seems to avoid you or dramas break out to prove otherwise. You're learning to be patient and introspective so that you can connect with the truth behind situations, and wake up spiritually. You can be self-centred and self-absorbed, so forcing yourself to deal with practical issues and everyday life can help to keep you grounded. You're an extremely clear communicator but your tone of voice may sometimes sound cutting because you can be blunt. You're learning to stand in others' shoes and to become more observant about the messages life is giving you.

# ALYSSA
## 1 3 7 1 1 1 = 14/5

Your goal is spiritual growth so you may take risks simply because they bring the most reward. But in your mind all experiences can be used as compost for your future. You generally have your head down reading books and you love words. Perhaps you're interested in acting, singing, marketing, journalism or research. You're a leader, but you're learning to apply elbow grease in order to manifest your ideas and vision. You enjoy finding out what makes people tick and you're fascinated by life. You're also learning to express yourself clearly, particularly emotionally in relationships.

# AMELIA
## 1 4 5 3 9 1  = 23/5

You may believe intelligence is based upon what you know and what you've learned in books. But true intelligence is based upon experience and there are no restrictions on how much you can learn and grow. You're sensual and sexual, and you may enjoy experimenting with perfumes and clothes that bring you to life. Sometimes you act or dress to thrill and you can be risqué, but you do know how far you can go without compromising your integrity. You love art, music and interior design. In business you may profit from others' knowledge, but you feel happier when you share the spoils of your success with others.

# AMY
## 1  4  7  = 12/3

You're a deep thinker, and spend much time pondering upon world issues, and how you can practically make a difference to life. For example, when everyone makes simple changes to their lifestyle with regards to recycling, it creates an enormous positive impact upon the environment, so you do your bit. You're gentle and caring, and you love nurturing those around you. Indeed you're forever busy fixing things, making things with your hands, or doing paperwork. Sometimes you're confused, disorganized and too laid back, but you're learning to focus. You love social get-togethers and you're very loyal to your friends.

# ANNA
## 1 5 5 1  = 12/3

You're deeply in contact with your soul and you use your mind, body and spirit to help you make sense of life. You give of yourself in every way, but at times you're unaware that it's time to stop and move onto other destinations. You're incredibly ambitious but you may give up your desires to help others. You can be self-critical, but even if you don't make 'A grade' you're learning to keep on going and stay on track. You're supremely self-confident, and you may be drawn to backpacking around the world for fun and entertainment. Life is for living, and you may be prepared to try almost anything that expands your experience and outlook on life.

# ASHLEY
## 1 1 8 3 5 7  =25/7

You're only motivated to get out of bed when there's something important or useful for you to do. For example, like playing in an important hockey match or working on a team project. You surround yourself with friends who support each other's growth, so your social anthropology skills may be helpful. You're popular and attractive, but you may suffer from an inferiority complex at times; you're learning to appreciate yourself. You may achieve recognition for your skills and attract gratitude from those you've helped along the way. You may be drawn towards spiritual and personal development because it helps you feel more connected to people and life.

# AVA
## 1 4 1  = 6

Sometimes you're a little angel, cute and sweet with a look like butter wouldn't melt in your mouth. At other times you're a little minx and you manipulate those around you to get what you want. You're a clever chick, but you may be tricky to understand because you can be a person of extremes. By learning to think of others you can help yourself to take the middle path and maintain a sense of equilibrium in your life. You're fascinated by different cultures but you're very traditional. You love music, flowers, love and romance, and all the good things in life. You're good at communicating your needs.

# CHARLOTTE
## 3 8 1 9 3 6 2 2 5  = 30/3

You may literally be ambidextrous, but at times your left hand doesn't know what your right hand's doing because you're the busiest bee. You flit in and out of people's lives whilst telling a joke and putting them at ease, and you always remember to leave before you outstay your welcome. You love the freedom to roam, and you may find intimate relationships stifling until you learn to relax and allow life to be. You may be drawn to spirituality, religion or politics, and meditation may help you to keep calm and centred. You're learning to express yourself fully.

# CHLOE
**3 8 3 6 5  = 25/7**

You're learning to question life and pay attention to the hidden meanings and messages the environment is giving you. You're psychic and intuitive, and you may use these tools to help others. You're waking up spiritually to a new level of awareness, and at times life feels very strange but you trust the process. You love to socialize, and this may play a big part in your working life. You have so many talents to choose from and that keep you busy. You enjoy analysing people, in a way that helps you learn more about yourself, but you reflect home truths to others too. You're learning to create emotional stability by using your powers of observation on yourself, and using your mind to rationalize.

# DAISY
**4 1 9 1 7  = 22/4**

You're always rearranging the furniture and putting things away into boxes because you may feel your survival depends on boundaries and structure. You function best with a set routine and you like to know exactly what's around the corner. You're learning to step out of the box and let go of rigidity, so you can experience expansion and growth. You're learning to resolve inner conflicts. You may create your own little empire where you can provide security for others. You're a good listener and offer reassurance to others. You're passionate about art, and you may invest in works of art for the future.

# ELIZABETH
5 3 9 8 1 2 5 2 8 = 43/7

Once you've made your mind up about something you need, then heaven and earth seem to move and suddenly it's created; this is the power of the spiritual creative will at work. You're also aware that on down days you can create havoc in equal measure, so you're learning to stay positive. You may be physically restless, which is a reflection of your state; meditation and yoga can help you to de-focus from the material world and find inner peace. You re-evaluate life often, and you learn to overcome obstacles by working harder. You recognize that life is what you make it.

# ELLA
5 3 3 1 = 12/3

You're learning to enjoy giving, so that even on days when you haven't even drunk a cup of coffee and your limbs are aching, you still carry on. You gain so much joy from helping others. You may be fussy and picky and notice even the tiniest detail that's out of place. You may take a long time with all your chores and activities because you like to do a thorough job. Sometimes you may want the world to run around you and treat you like a queen – because of all that you do and all that you've done for everyone. You're good at letting your hair down, and you're good at recognizing when it's time to move on to new opportunities. You're a busy bee who makes the most of each day.

# EMILY
## 5 4 9 3 7 = 28/10/1

You're like a little Peter Pan who's learning to grow up and face reality. Perhaps you've been very spoiled and are used to getting your own way; when people say 'no' it may shock you into stunned silence. You're incredibly inventive and are able to find solutions to most problems. You possess the drive to go for your goals fearlessly and full on. You're learning to stand on your own two feet and you may be pleasantly surprised by how strong you can be; you can also be a tower of strength to others. Once you've found your motivation you're off making a success of life. You're a real pioneer.

# EMMA
## 5 4 4 1 = 14/5

You possess an alluring voice, and you draw people into your world until they are hooked and can't get enough. You weave a web of fascination by keeping people guessing and you give little away. You're a deep thinker and your mind is often elsewhere. You're highly capable and self-reliant, but you can be proud, and you're learning to be more down to earth. You're good at research and writing. You particularly enjoy studying when you know it can contribute towards a qualification, towards you earning a living, or because it may improve your status or popularity.

# EVIE
5 4 9 5 = 23/5

You're a great friend to have around because you're always willing to speak your mind and tell the truth. You find it impossible to lie because you know it will come back and bite you. You're street-wise and people value your wisdom, but you're learning to be more tolerant towards those without degrees or your acquired level of knowledge. You're always on the go but you're learning to create a stable environment where you can feel safe to explore your heart and soul. Embarking upon deep and meaningful relationships may be one good way to overcome your 'fear of flying' or close attachment.

# GRACE
7 9 1 3 5 = 25/7

You're a perfectionist and only the best is good enough for you. However, you may experience a fall from grace if you take yourself too seriously. You're learning to be more realistic about life. You're a catalyst and you spark off change wherever you go, but you've realized the importance of using this gift responsibly. Finding out the truth is imperative to you; you're always delving into situations discovering new facts even when there appear to be no more to uncover. You're learning to make sense of life by reaching inwards to your soul for clarity because then you can see the bigger picture.

# HANNAH
## 8 1 5 5 1 8  = 28/10/1

You may excel in business or in the communications field, but you're learning to acquire people skills in order to progress your talents. You're proud of your own strengths but you may fear failure; everyone makes mistakes so welcome constructive feedback to help you move forwards. You may be compulsive and dive into situations without knowing the details, but this provides you with plenty of fodder for self-analysis. You may be very intellectual and detached at times; you're learning to engage your heart and soul to help you lead a happy and fulfilled life.

# ISABELLA
## 9 1 1 2 5 3 3 1  = 25/7

You're interested in the deeper issues in life; philosophy, psychology and spirituality. You spend a great deal of time searching out people who can expand your awareness of the cosmos and the world because to you knowledge is king. You're extremely sensitive to pain, and you may run a mile from a situation if you feel you're going to get burnt emotionally. At times you feel as though you don't fit in, but this may be due to you isolating yourself or losing touch with reality. You're learning to apply common sense to situations, and to look to your intuition for guidance and clarity.

# ISABELLE
## 9 1 1 2 5 3 3 5  = 29/11/2

You're attracted to all the fine things in life: art, music, literature, cordon bleu food, antiques, theatre and film. You're also inspired by all the great minds that have walked the earth. Your desire for knowledge is insatiable. You may be fragile emotionally, but you're learning to push yourself beyond your limits in order to make a success of your life. As long as you're experiencing spiritual growth you're happy; you enjoy passing on your wisdom to others. You can be temperamental at times and you're learning to do what's best rather than focusing on your personal desires all the time; look to your soul for inspiration.

# ISLA
## 9 1 3 1  = 14/5

You're an ideas person, but you may give away your great inventions to others, who ride with them and blossom with success. You're a people person, but you prefer to analyse from a distance rather than surrounding yourself with a crowd. You like meaty projects, and working through issues that lead you on a journey deep into your soul. You're happy to embrace change even if it means moving to the other side of the world, and you're always changing your attitude to life. You may possess psychic powers but your scientific brain helps you to recognize the truth when you see it. You're learning to make sense of life.

## JASMINE
1 1 1 4 9 5 5 = 26/8

You're a whizz at delivering potent messages, and you're willing to stir people up if that's what's needed in order for them to get your meaning. You're also learning to use your gifts responsibly. You're charming and witty and you may bowl people over with your blatant inner strength – nothing seems to faze you. You like to surround yourself with people who can stand up to your boldness (and your ego). You're extremely competitive, but you do enjoy sharing the limelight with team achievements. You're learning to develop a strong sense of community and to be kind and considerate towards others.

## JESSICA
1 5 1 1 9 3 1 = 21/3

Your whole existence revolves around your family and friends, and like a swarm of bees you huddle together merrily going about your job. Teamwork is your ideal. You're learning to find your place in the group so that you can become the most effective, and be of use. Sometimes you give too much or are needy for attention; you're learning to focus your attention back on yourself. You may involve yourself too readily in others' situations and you're learning to wait to be asked for help. You create so many distractions when there's something you do not want to do, but you're learning to concentrate, and to get on with the job and follow through.

# KATIE
## 2 1 2 9 5  = 19/10/1

You like to be the boss and as long as everyone around you is clear on this position, all is well. You're learning to be guided by your soul, the big boss, and to be humble and accept that deep down everyone is equal. Your mind rules the roost and you see life as it is in the cold light of day, but you're learning to find intimacy so that it all feels real. You're wise and worldly but you value naïvety; it refreshes your outlook on life at times when you feel jaded because you've seen it all. You're a pioneer of new inventions, and you're learning to focus on your goals.

# LARA
## 3 1 9 1  = 14/5

You're incredibly popular, and your wide circle of friends includes people of all ages and backgrounds because you get along with everyone. You're ambitious, and you generally achieve top marks because you simply must prove your knowledge. You want to be accepted but you earn your pat on the back. You enjoy being centrestage but you're learning to be inspired by others' success too. You love flowers, music, parties and studying, because you want to discover more about life. You may be prone to addictions (exercise, sex, chocolate, work, etc.), but you're learning to use your mind to rationalize so that you do what you need to do, rather than what you want.

# LEAH
## 3 5 1 8 = 17/8

You're learning to trust your intuition, and to walk your talk. There is presence about you because you are so deeply connected to your soul and to life. You're strong, purposeful and direct and you take no nonsense from others. At times you can be over-imaginative or exaggerate facts, but you're learning to recognize fact from fiction. You enjoy quiet times and sometimes you keep friends and family at a distance, but you're learning not to isolate yourself. You're also learning to feel comfortable being a part of the group where you can find strength, love and support.

# LEYLA
## 3 5 7 3 1 = 19/10/1

You're a forward-thinking person but what makes you so directional is that you can see behind you too. You're able to recognize where you've been before, which helps you to avoid pitfalls. You enjoy intellectual pursuits; you're constantly picking others' brains because you like to polish your skills at general knowledge. Sometimes you're frustrated by simple things, like loading new software onto your computer, but obstacles are there for you to overcome and you're happy to persevere on your own until the job's done. You're creative and expressive and you certainly shout if you're hurt. You're learning to re-evaluate life so that you can do even better.

# LILY
## 3 9 3 7  = 22/4

You're open and intuitive and your mind is receptive to new ideas. This may be at odds with your body that's saying stay safe, stick with what you know and what you've got. You may be gloriously content with the material life you've created but there's so much more potential; you're learning to explore many gifts in this lifetime. By utilizing your talents you may provide a springboard for others to be able to journey more deeply into life. You're learning to endure the dark times because you know they lead you closer to your soul. You crave peace and harmony in life; you're a peacemaker at heart.

# LUCY
## 3 3 3 7  = 16/7

You're happy-go-lucky. You possess a comical sense of humour and enjoy imitating people with such uncanny accuracy that even they find amusing. Your home may be a sanctuary for those who need a rest away from the stresses of everyday life. You enjoy cooking and entertaining, but when you close your door you expect people to honour your space. You can be emotionally abusive at times, especially when you feel hurt or wounded by a situation or through misunderstanding. You're learning to heal emotional hurts and let go of the past by reflecting on how you react in difficult situations. You're learning to trust yourself and the process of life.

## MACKENZIE
4 1 3 2 5 5 8 9 5  = 42/6

You're practical and efficient, and you're always trying to identify ways to improve life for others. For example, by monitoring the performance of your vehicle and servicing it regularly to ensure that your journey runs smoothly. You're interested in fundamental rules and regulations, and you like to ensure your team is run by fairness. You may be at the very heart of an organization, and from an early age show a deep caring towards others' needs. You're offended by greed because to you when someone takes too much it means others will have to go without; fairness is key. However, you're learning to be compassionate and to accept that people are learning different lessons in life.

## MADELYN
4 1 4 5 3 7 5  = 29/11/2

You've a lightness of spirit that people find uplifting and comforting. You're extremely sensitive and vulnerable at times, but your receptive nature brings people close together. You like reading autobiographies of interesting people. You aspire to use your talents and live up to your highest potential. Rome wasn't built in a day and you're learning to persevere with your goals and enjoy each step of your journey. You possess simple taste in clothes and decoration, but you're learning to experiment occasionally in order to spice up your life. You're practical and tend to choose whom you allow yourself to fall in love with carefully.

# MADISON
4 1 4 9 1 6 5  = 30/3

You're prolifically creative, and you constantly busy yourself with a variety of daily activities. You're learning to centre yourself and find stillness in your life so that you can become even more productive. You're fascinated by religion and politics, and interested in social issues; you love listening to people's different opinions but you voice your beliefs too. You enjoy light-hearted gossip but you may easily get carried away with careless talk. You're learning to observe your thoughts and words, and to take responsibility for yourself. You generally follow through on your commitments and can create tangible results in life. You're confident and you breeze through life by taking it all in your stride.

# MARIA
4 1 9 9 1  = 24/6

You possess a strong sense of family and duty and you're community spirited. You're good at managing your finances and you're able to nurture yourself and bond with others. You tend to see life through rose-coloured spectacles but you're learning to come down to earth and face reality. Hard work is the usual means for success, and by applying yourself you may well be able to secure many of your goals. You can be sulky and wilful at times; you're learning to cooperate because it's the fastest route to productivity and harmony. You're warm, loving and generous, and you may fall in love easily.

# MATILDA
## 4 1 2 9 3 4 1  = 24/6

You want to create a nice, quiet life, where the sun always shines and the sea is guarded safely by a gentle breeze, as you eat sumptuous delights and rest in the heavens. You can easily become complacent so you're learning to get up, get out, and get on with life. Sometimes you dig your heels in and refuse to budge. Life is littered with short, sharp shocks and pleasant surprises that move you on regardless. You're learning to accept that everything happens for a reason and that ultimately it works out for the best. You may love fashion, photography and the piano, and you're devoted to your family and friends. You love to get involved with your community.

# MIA
## 4 9 1  = 14/5

You use your gifts to make a tangible difference to life and you aim to stamp your imprint on the world by leaving it in a better state than when you arrived. However, your world is right here, right now, and you can make a difference simply by taking responsibility for your life. You're headstrong and you like to get your own way, but you may possess radical beliefs or opinions that are limiting your experiences. You're learning to accept that life moves on and situations do change; be open to new ideas so that you can progress in life. Communicate.

# MILLY
## 4 9 3 3 7  = 26/8

You're an ambitious little cookie, and you take your studies seriously because you believe that knowledge is the key to success. You're strong-willed and if you set your mind to something, you believe you can achieve it, and often you do. At times you argue with those in authority but you're learning to assert your personal power and to find your own path in life. You're hard-working and reliable and you may enjoy responsibilities. You find enjoyment in the simple pleasures in life. You're learning to connect with your spirituality in order to discover inner peace and satisfaction.

# NADIA
## 5 1 4 9 1  = 20/2

You're an earth mother and a spiritual goddess, and you're always trying to balance these two very different aspects of yourself in life. You're constantly measuring up situations to see where you fit in and how they can be of use to you, and you take time weighing up before making important decisions. You need reassurance that you're loved and wanted, and you want to know that people are going to be nice to you before you let them in (emotionally). Sometimes you can be overcautious and manipulate situations to avoid feeling rejected. You're learning to stop taking life so personally. You're kind, and people may come to you for counselling.

## NATALIE
5 1 2 1 3 9 5 = 26/8

You're a strong person, but you may be scared of your power. Perhaps you fear you may misuse it or inadvertently hurt someone along the way. You're very caring and protective, but you're learning to guide others by empowering them to make their own decisions in life. You're a spiritual warrior waking up to truth, but you fully respect that others have the right to choose their own path in life. Occasionally you throw tantrums, which can be explosive, but you do not bear grudges. You're learning to recognize the effect your energy has on your environment, and also to take responsibility for your role in materializing the world.

## OLIVIA
6 3 9 4 9 1 = 32/5

You're dutiful and serious about your responsibilities, but you'd like to feel free of your commitments sometimes. You love sailing, skiing, riding and chess, and indeed anything that challenges you to use your brain and stamina to the max. You like organizing social events, like fund-raising or weddings, as long as they are for a good purpose. You can be overly fussy and superficial, and you're learning to judge people by their actions rather than by what they say. You want continuity in your life; at times you cling on to loved ones for security. You're learning to value yourself and your abilities. You're affectionate, popular and creative.

# POPPY
## 9 6 7 7 7  =36/9

You're surrounded by love and this inspires your creativity. You may write poetry, draw beautiful paintings, or use your energy campaigning for human rights. You're a mover and a shaker and you like to see justice is done. You can be argumentative, and easily annoyed by trivialities, but you're learning to relax. You can be shy and withdrawn, and may judge yourself harshly; you're learning to be nice to yourself. You are a daydreamer, but this may help inspire you to manifest your dreams. Your never-ending resourcefulness is an inspiration to others, and it also serves you well.

# RANIA
## 9 1 5 9 1  = 25/7

You may lead a hyperactive lifestyle and pack as much into a day as others fit into a week. You like things done yesterday, and whilst you can design your own agenda and tend to pressurize others for results, you're learning to be more relaxed. You're insightful and you're able to paint a clear picture to verbally illustrate your intentions. People may think you're 'off with the faeries' (perhaps because some of your ideas are so new), but you're learning to be yourself and let life flow. You generally get along with everyone but you're learning to speak your truth.

## RUBY
### 9 3 2 7 = 21/3

The only way you can be clear about your long-term commitments and intentions is by learning to recognize who you are and what 'job' you need to do. You're strong-willed and emotionally unstable at times and you may be thrown off course by life's events. You're learning to recognize that it's 'god's will' or your soul that ultimately guides you through life and helps you to do what's best. You're often the centre of attention; you're a loving soul with a great sense of humour and always have a good word for everyone. You're full of joy that lights up your life and brings hope to others.

## SAMANTHA
### 1 1 4 1 5 2 8 1 = 23/5

You aim to lift yourself up out of the monotony of everyday life by using your creativity. You're inspired when you are being creative, and whether it's baking a cake or painting an intricate oil painting, you give it one hundred per cent. You can be scatterbrained at times, and take on too much so that life slips through your fingers. You're learning to pay attention to what you're doing and to become more reliable. You're a traveller in every sense of the word and you're spontaneous, so life is always exciting when you're around. You do not tolerate complacency because you're a powerful agent for change, and that means effort and activity.

# SARA
## 1 1 9 1 = 12/3

You're generally easy-going, but when you or your loved ones are rattled by life's little injustices your temper rises and you're a force to be reckoned with. People run scared of your tongue as you're so expressive, and you spare no blushes when it comes to telling the truth. You're learning to be thoughtful when you're putting people in the picture so that they are more receptive to working things out. Your creativity is inspirational, and you like to constantly make things with your hands. You enjoy regular chats and a coffee with friends, but your parties are legendary! You're learning to be optimistic about life and also to make the most of every day.

# SARAH
## 1 1 9 1 8 = 20/2

You set yourself high standards; you're a pleaser and you work hard to live up to people's expectations. You want to get it right but you're scared of being rejected; you're learning to listen to your intuition for guidance. Sometimes a battle rages between your mind and emotions and you may find it difficult to make decisions. Perhaps you try to manipulate a resolution to a situation or try to force an answer. You're using the wisdom you've gained from all your past experiences to help you create a brighter future. You're motherly and warm, and possess a gentleness that welcomes people to you with open arms. You're a great listener and a compassionate companion in life.

## SIENNA
### 1 9 5 5 5 1 = 26/8

For you life is an open and closed shop where you make all the important decisions yourself, and people can think what they want. Yes, you are in charge of the ship but your sails are governed by the spiritual law of justice; there may be surprises in store if you keep battling against your higher will. You may be gifted with languages and you're a plain speaker. You're learning to open up emotionally with loved ones, and to listen to what they say when they're offering you good advice. You enjoy making money, but you're learning to be resilient during lean times and manage your resources because you like to live well.

## SOPHIA
### 1 6 7 8 9 1 = 32/5

You're a loving person, with a good heart; you really want the best for people. Whilst you're intelligent, outgoing and adventurous, people can sometimes be surprised by your naïvety. You may allow yourself to be used because it's easier than kicking up a fuss, or because you can see behind the situation. You're learning to speak up for your rights and to stop making excuses for others. You're ambitious, and you forge your path ahead with momentum and vigour. You're more than capable of earning a good living, which is just as well because you possess expensive taste.

## SOPHIE
**1 6 7 8 9 5 = 36/9**

You possess a regal air about you, mainly because you're so confident and possess outstandingly good manners; perhaps you're the result of selective breeding. Your life is governed by your desire to live up to others' expectations. For example, to attain entrance grades to the best school or to hold a leading role in society. You may feel overprotected at times, and rebelliously try to break away from tradition. You believe you can get what you want in life and sometimes you may act like a little princess – you want it all. You're learning to be adaptable, compassionate, and to accept when you've done your best.

## ZOE
**8 6 5 = 19/10/1**

You're waking up to your spirituality, and you're learning how to use your personal power to assert your individuality and go for your goals. You may feel like a victim at times because you can be naïve, but you're growing up and taking responsibility for your life. You realize it's up to you to be strong and to say, 'no' if you do feel like you're being used. You're worldly and wise, and you're learning to live in accordance with your values. People may be inspired by your gifts. You may be drawn to the world of business or to helping humanitarian causes. You may possess visionary skills.

Chapter 9

# The Top 1,000 Baby Names of the Century So Far

This section contains a list of the UK's top 1,000 girls' and boys' names for the years 2000 to 2010, just in case you need some inspiration. The names which are discussed in detail in Chapter 8, '100 Popular Baby Names', are marked with an asterisk.

# Top 500 Girls' Names

| | | |
|---|---|---|
| Aaliyah | Aliyah | *Anna |
| Abby | Allie | Annabelle |
| *Abigail | Allison | Anne |
| *Addison | Allyson | Annie |
| Addyson | Alondra | Annika |
| Adriana | Alyson | Anya |
| Adrianna | *Alyssa | April |
| Alaina | Amanda | Ariana |
| Alana | Amari | Arianna |
| Alanna | Amaya | Ariel |
| Alayna | Amber | Ashanti |
| Alejandra | *Amelia | Ashlee |
| Alexa | *Amy | Ashleigh |
| Alexandra | Ana | *Ashley |
| Alexandria | Anahi | Ashlyn |
| Alexia | Anastasia | Ashlynn |
| *Alexis | Andrea | Asia |
| Alice | Angel | Athena |
| Alicia | Angela | Aubrey |
| Alina | Angelica | Audrey |
| Alisha | Angelina | Aurora |
| Alison | Angie | Autumn |
| Alissa | Aniya | *Ava |
| Alivia | Aniyah | Avery |

| | | |
|---|---|---|
| Ayanna | Carla | Crystal |
| Bailey | Carly | Cynthia |
| Bella | Carmen | *Daisy |
| Bethany | Carolina | Dakota |
| Bianca | Caroline | Dana |
| Breanna | Carolyn | Daniela |
| Brenda | Casey | Daniella |
| Brenna | Cassandra | Danielle |
| Briana | Cassidy | Deanna |
| Brianna | Catherine | Delaney |
| Bridget | Cecilia | Delilah |
| Brielle | Celeste | Denise |
| Britney | *Charlotte | Desiree |
| Brittany | Chelsea | Destinee |
| Brittney | Cheyanne | Destiny |
| Brooke | Cheyenne | Diamond |
| Brooklyn | *Chloe | Diana |
| Brooklynn | Christina | Dominique |
| Bryanna | Christine | Dulce |
| Brynn | Ciara | Eden |
| Cadence | Cierra | Elaina |
| Caitlin | Cindy | Eleanor |
| Caitlyn | Claire | Elena |
| Callie | Clara | Eliana |
| Cameron | Clarissa | Elisabeth |
| Camila | Claudia | Elise |
| Camille | Cora | Eliza |
| Camryn | Courtney | *Elizabeth |
| Cara | Cristina | *Ella |

| | | |
|---|---|---|
| Ellie | Gloria | Itzel |
| Emely | *Grace | Ivy |
| Emerson | Gracie | Izabella |
| Emilee | Hailee | Jacqueline |
| Emilia | Hailey | Jada |
| *Emily | Haleigh | Jade |
| *Emma | Haley | Jaden |
| Erica | Halle | Jadyn |
| Erika | Hallie | Jaelyn |
| Erin | Hanna | Jamie |
| Esmeralda | *Hannah | Jane |
| Esther | Harley | Janelle |
| Estrella | Harmony | Janiya |
| Eva | Hayden | Jaqueline |
| Evelyn | Haylee | Jasmin |
| *Evie | Hayley | *Jasmine |
| Faith | Heather | Jayda |
| Fatima | Heaven | Jayden |
| Fernanda | Heidi | Jayla |
| Fiona | Helen | Jazmin |
| Francesca | Holly | Jazmine |
| Gabriela | Hope | Jenna |
| Gabriella | Imani | Jennifer |
| Gabrielle | India | Jenny |
| Genesis | Iris | *Jessica |
| Genevieve | Isabel | Jillian |
| Georgia | *Isabella | Joanna |
| Gianna | *Isabelle | Jocelyn |
| Giselle | *Isla | Johanna |

| | | |
|---|---|---|
| Jordan | *Katie | Kylie |
| Jordyn | Katrina | Kyra |
| Joselyn | Kaydence | Lacey |
| Josephine | Kayla | Laila |
| Josie | Kaylee | *Lara |
| Julia | Kayleigh | Laura |
| Juliana | Kaylie | Lauren |
| Julianna | Kaylin | Lauryn |
| Julie | Keira | Layla |
| Julissa | Kelly | *Leah |
| Kaelyn | Kelsey | Leila |
| Kailey | Kendall | Leilani |
| Kaitlin | Kendra | Lena |
| Kaitlyn | Kennedy | Leslie |
| Kaitlynn | Khloe | Lesly |
| Kaleigh | Kiana | *Leyla |
| Kamryn | Kiara | Lexi |
| Kara | Kiera | Lila |
| Karen | Kiley | Liliana |
| Karina | Kimberly | Lillian |
| Karla | Kira | Lilly |
| Kassandra | Kirsten | *Lily |
| Kassidy | Kristen | Linda |
| Kate | Kristin | Lindsay |
| Katelyn | Kristina | Lindsey |
| Katelynn | Krystal | Lisa |
| Katherine | Kyla | Lizbeth |
| Kathleen | Kylee | Logan |
| Kathryn | Kyleigh | Lola |

| | | |
|---|---|---|
| London | Martha | *Natalie |
| Lucia | Mary | Natasha |
| *Lucy | *Matilda | Nayeli |
| Lydia | Maya | Nevaeh |
| Macie | Mckenna | Nia |
| *Mackenzie | Mckenzie | Nicole |
| Macy | Megan | Nina |
| Madalyn | Meghan | Noelle |
| Maddison | Melanie | Nora |
| Madeleine | Melissa | Nyla |
| Madeline | Melody | *Olivia |
| *Madelyn | Mercedes | Paige |
| Madilyn | Meredith | Paola |
| *Madison | *Mia | Paris |
| Maggie | Michaela | Patricia |
| Makayla | Michelle | Paulina |
| Makenna | Mikayla | Payton |
| Malia | *Milly | Perla |
| Mallory | Miracle | Peyton |
| Margaret | Miranda | Phoebe |
| *Maria | Miriam | Piper |
| Mariah | Molly | *Poppy |
| Mariana | Monica | Presley |
| Marie | Morgan | Priscilla |
| Marina | Mya | Rachael |
| Marisa | *Nadia | Rachel |
| Marisol | Nancy | Raegan |
| Marissa | Naomi | *Rania |
| Marley | Natalia | Raquel |

| | | |
|---|---|---|
| Raven | Shania | Tiana |
| Reagan | Shannon | Tiffany |
| Rebecca | Shayla | Tori |
| Rebekah | Shelby | Trinity |
| Reese | Sidney | Valentina |
| Regan | *Sienna | Valeria |
| Riley | Sierra | Valerie |
| Rosa | Skye | Vanessa |
| Rose | Skylar | Veronica |
| *Ruby | Skyler | Victoria |
| Ruth | Sofia | Violet |
| Rylee | *Sophia | Virginia |
| Ryleigh | *Sophie | Vivian |
| Rylie | Stella | Viviana |
| Sabrina | Stephanie | Wendy |
| Sadie | Summer | Whitney |
| Sage | Sydney | Ximena |
| *Samantha | Tabitha | Yasmin |
| Sandra | Talia | Yesenia |
| *Sara | Tamia | *Zoe |
| *Sarah | Tania | Zoey |
| Sarai | Tara | |
| Sasha | Taryn | |
| Savanna | Tatiana | |
| Savannah | Tatum | |
| Scarlett | Taylor | |
| Selena | Teagan | |
| Serena | Teresa | |
| Serenity | Tessa | |

# Top 500 Boys' Names

| | | |
|---|---|---|
| Aaron | Amari | Billy |
| Abel | Amir | *Blake |
| Abraham | Anderson | Bobby |
| *Adam | Andre | Braden |
| Adan | Andres | Bradley |
| Aden | *Andrew | Brady |
| Adrian | Andy | Braeden |
| Ahmad | Angel | Branden |
| Aidan | Angelo | Brandon |
| *Aiden | *Anthony | Braxton |
| Alan | Antonio | Brayan |
| Albert | Armando | Brayden |
| Alberto | Arthur | Braydon |
| Alec | Arturo | Braylon |
| Alejandro | Asher | Brendan |
| Alex | Ashton | Brenden |
| *Alexander | Austin | Brendon |
| Alexis | Avery | Brennan |
| *Alfie | Axel | Brent |
| Alfredo | Ayden | Brett |
| Ali | Bailey | Brian |
| Allan | Beau | Brock |
| Allen | *Benjamin | Brody |
| Alvin | Bennett | Bruce |

| | | |
|---|---|---|
| Bryan | Clayton | Darren |
| Bryant | Cody | *David |
| Bryce | Colby | Davis |
| Bryson | Cole | Dawson |
| Byron | Colin | Dean |
| Cade | Collin | Deandre |
| Caden | Colton | Declan |
| Caiden | Conner | Demetrius |
| Caleb | *Connor | Dennis |
| Calvin | Conor | Derek |
| Camden | *Cooper | Derrick |
| Cameron | Corbin | Desmond |
| Carl | Corey | Devin |
| Carlos | Cory | Devon |
| Carson | Craig | Diego |
| Carter | Cristian | Dillon |
| Casey | Cruz | Dominic |
| Cash | Curtis | Dominick |
| Cayden | Dakota | Donald |
| Cesar | Dallas | Donovan |
| Chad | Dalton | Dorian |
| Chance | Damian | Douglas |
| Chandler | Damien | Drake |
| Charles | Damon | Drew |
| *Charlie | Dane | Dustin |
| Chase | *Daniel | *Dylan |
| Chris | Danny | Eddie |
| *Christian | Dante | Edgar |
| *Christopher | Darius | Eduardo |

| | | |
|---|---|---|
| Edward | Franklin | Hunter |
| Edwin | Frederick | Ian |
| Eli | *Gabriel | Isaac |
| Elias | Gael | Isaiah |
| Elijah | Gage | Isiah |
| Elliot | Garrett | Ismael |
| Elliott | Gary | Israel |
| Emanuel | Gavin | Issac |
| Emiliano | *George | *Ivan |
| Emilio | Gerald | *Jack |
| Emmanuel | Gerardo | Jackson |
| Enrique | Giovanni | *Jacob |
| Eric | Grady | Jaden |
| Erick | Graham | Jadon |
| Erik | Grant | Jaiden |
| Ernesto | Grayson | Jaime |
| Esteban | Gregory | *Jake |
| *Ethan | Griffin | Jakob |
| Evan | Guillermo | Jalen |
| Everett | Gustavo | Jamal |
| Ezekiel | Harrison | Jamari |
| Ezra | *Harry | *James |
| Fabian | *Harvey | Jameson |
| Felipe | Hayden | Jared |
| Felix | Hector | Jarrett |
| Fernando | Henry | Jason |
| *Finlay | Holden | Jasper |
| Francisco | Hudson | Javier |
| Frank | Hugo | Javon |

| | | |
|---|---|---|
| Jaxson | Jonathon | Khalil |
| Jay | Jordan | Kobe |
| Jayce | Jorge | Kody |
| *Jayden | Jose | Kristian |
| Jaydon | *Joseph | Kristopher |
| Jaylen | *Joshua | Kyle |
| Jaylin | Josiah | Kyler |
| Jaylon | Josue | *Lachlan |
| Jayson | Juan | Lance |
| Jeffery | Jude | Landen |
| Jeffrey | Julian | Landon |
| Jeremiah | Julio | Lane |
| Jeremy | Julius | Larry |
| Jermaine | Justice | Lawrence |
| Jerry | Justin | Leo |
| Jesse | Kade | Leonardo |
| Jessie | Kaden | Leonel |
| Jesus | Kai | Levi |
| Jimmy | Kaiden | *Liam |
| Joaquin | Kaleb | Lincoln |
| Joe | Kameron | *Logan |
| Joel | Kayden | Lorenzo |
| *John | Keaton | Louis |
| Johnathan | Keegan | Luca |
| Johnny | Keith | *Lucas |
| Jon | Kelvin | Luis |
| Jonah | Kenneth | Lukas |
| nas | Kenny | Luke |
| athan | Kevin | Maddox |

| | | |
|---|---|---|
| Malachi | Miles | Paul |
| Malcolm | Mitchell | Payton |
| Malik | *Mohammed | Pedro |
| Manuel | Moises | *Peter |
| Marc | Morgan | Peyton |
| Marco | Moses | Philip |
| Marcos | Myles | Phillip |
| Marcus | Nasir | Preston |
| Mario | *Nathan | Quentin |
| Mark | Nathanael | Quincy |
| Marshall | Nathaniel | Quinn |
| Martin | Nehemiah | Quinton |
| Marvin | Nelson | Rafael |
| Mason | *Nicholas | Ramon |
| Mateo | Nickolas | Randy |
| Mathew | Nicolas | Raul |
| *Matthew | Nikolas | Raymond |
| Maurice | *Noah | Reece |
| Mauricio | Noe | Reed |
| *Max | Noel | Reese |
| Maximilian | Nolan | Reginald |
| Maximus | *Oliver | Reid |
| Maxwell | Omar | Rene |
| Mekhi | Orlando | Ricardo |
| Melvin | Oscar | Richard |
| Micah | Owen | Ricky |
| *Michael | Pablo | *Riley |
| Micheal | Parker | *Robert |
| Miguel | Patrick | Roberto |

| | | |
|---|---|---|
| Rodney | Skyler | Tyson |
| Rodrigo | Solomon | Uriel |
| Roger | Spencer | Victor |
| Roman | Stephen | Vincent |
| Ronald | Steve | Walker |
| Rowan | Steven | Walter |
| Roy | Tanner | Wesley |
| Ruben | Tate | Weston |
| Russell | Taylor | *William |
| *Ryan | Terrance | Willie |
| Ryder | Terrell | Wyatt |
| Rylan | Terry | Xander |
| Salvador | Theodore | Xavier |
| Sam | *Thomas | Yahir |
| Samuel | Timothy | Zachariah |
| Santiago | Tommy | Zachary |
| Saul | Tony | Zachery |
| Sawyer | Travis | Zackary |
| Scott | Trent | Zackery |
| Sean | Trenton | Zander |
| Sebastian | Trevon | Zane |
| Sergio | Trevor | Zion |
| Seth | Trey | |
| Shane | Tristan | |
| Shaun | Tristen | |
| Shawn | Troy | |
| Silas | Tucker | |
| *Simon | Ty | |
| Skylar | Tyler | |

# Resources

## Professional Contacts

Association International de Numerologues (AIN) is the international body governing Numerology. To book a reading with a professional Numerologist, or for information on workshops, professional training, or events worldwide, please visit the website: www.numerologyworld.org.